Management is NOT Manipulation

Beyond the Illusion: Authentic Leadership for Sustainable Success

By

Mitash Bhattacharyya

MBA, ALP-IIMA

Copyright © 2024 Mitash Bhattacharyya

- All rights reserved.

Copy of this book cannot be replicated for any commercial or professional training purpose without prior permission from the author.

Disclaimer: This book does not claim that every data and statistics sacrosanct as because they are all dynamic in nature and will vary from time to time

Edited By
Anuradha Bhattacharyya & Anumita Bhattacharjee

DEDICATED TO

CORPORATE LEADERSHIP GLOBALLY

Preface

In the complex and fast-paced world of business, management is often viewed as the art of achieving results, leading people, and ensuring organizational success. Yet, an alarming trend has emerged—manipulation masquerading as management. This trend not only undermines the principles of ethical leadership but also jeopardizes the very foundations of organizational sustainability.

The genesis of this book lies in a simple observation: organizations that prioritize short-term gains through unethical practices often suffer long-term consequences. From manipulated data influencing critical decisions to toxic cultures fuelled by favouritism and lack of accountability, the ripple effects of such behaviours extend far beyond individual failures—they harm the collective success of businesses, employees, and stakeholders alike.

This book explores the critical distinction between management and manipulation. It delves into the subtle but destructive ways in which data, processes, and people are misused under the guise of leadership. Drawing on real-world examples, proven frameworks, and actionable strategies, the book highlights how organizations can avoid the pitfalls of unethical practices.

Central to the discussion is the need for ethical leadership and robust organizational governance. Through frameworks like the FITT (Fund, Infrastructure, Technology, Talent) model and tools such as the Balanced Scorecard and Net Promoter Score, this book offers practical guidance for building cultures of integrity, transparency, and accountability.

Whether you are a seasoned CEO, a rising manager, or an HR professional shaping workplace policy, this book serves as both a guide and a call to action. It challenges leaders to rethink how decisions are made, how talent is managed, and how success is measured—not just in terms of profitability but also in terms of long-term sustainability and ethical governance.

Management is not about manipulation. It is about planning, organizing, leading, and controlling with purpose and integrity. It is about fostering a work environment where honesty is rewarded, talent is nurtured, and decisions are guided by data-driven truth rather than convenient fiction.

As you turn the pages of this book, my hope is that it will inspire you to embrace ethical leadership, transform your organizational culture, and contribute to a future where businesses thrive not because of manipulation, but in spite of it.

Mitash Bhattacharyya
Author

Visit : *www.augustalent.com*

Table of Contents

Chapter 1: The Illusion of Success Through Manipulation 6
    The Illusion of Success Through Manipulation 6
    Understanding manipulation in management 19
    How data forging starts the chain of bad decisions 28
    Case studies: Organizations that suffered due to manipulated analytics 31

Chapter 2: Ethics and Accountability in Decision-Making 33
    Ethics and Accountability in Decision-Making 33
    Why ethics matter in management practices 35
    The ripple effect of unethical practices on Organizational Culture 37
    Developing accountability frameworks to prevent manipulation 39

Chapter 3: Organizational Culture Audits 43
    Role of HR in identifying 46
    Cultural and Operational GAPS 46
    Conducting effective culture audits: 53
    Tools and Techniques 53
    Addressing root causes of Toxicity and Turnover 57

Chapter 4: The FITT Business Model 64
    Fund: Avoiding Valuation inflation and 67
    Financial Mismanagement 67
    Infrastructure: Strategic balance between 69
    Online and Offline systems 69
    Technology: The cost of resisting innovation 71
    Talent: Building competency frameworks for Recruitment and Training 74

Chapter 5: Managing Talent Ethically 77

Developing Competency Frameworks with Behavioural Indicators 80

The Role of Mentoring and Coaching for 86

Organizational Success 86

Addressing nepotism and favouritism in 92

Talent Management 92

Chapter 6: The Role of Leadership in Ethical Management 97

How CEOs and Top Management influence 101

Culture and Sustainability 101

Choosing and Training CEOs: Building a new Competency Model 105

Transitioning from Functional Leadership to Organizational Leadership 110

Chapter 7: Governance and ESG Integration 115

Aligning management practices with 124

ESG Principles 124

Sustainable Decision-Making for 128

Long-Term Profitability 128

Creating Governance Frameworks to ensure 132

Ethical Leadership 132

Chapter 8: Tools and Processes for Balanced Decision-Making 137

Tools and Processes for Balanced Decision-Making 137

The Olympic Business Model: Balancing Qualitative and Quantitative factors 142

Leveraging the Balanced Scorecard for 152

Strategic Alignment 152

Using NPS and VOC analysis for 155

Continuous Improvement 155

Chapter 9: Re-Skilling and Future-Proofing Talent 158

- Identifying Skill Gaps and 161
- Creating Development Pathways 161
- Building a culture of continuous 166
- Learning and Innovation 166
- Examples of successful 174
- Talent Transformation Programs 174

Chapter 10: Building a Legacy of Ethical Management 179
- Developing a culture admired for 183
- Integrity and Maturity 183
- Ensuring profitability and sustainability through Ethical Governance 192
- Inspiring Future Leaders to Redefine 196
- Management without Manipulation 196

Epilogue: The Path to Sustainable Success 205
- Reflecting on the True Purpose of Management 207
- A call to action for Leaders, HR professionals, and Stakeholders 210

Chapter 1: The Illusion of Success Through Manipulation

Understanding manipulation in management

How data forging starts the chain of bad decisions

Case studies: Organizations that suffered due to manipulated analytics

The Illusion of Success Through Manipulation

Management, at its core, is about fostering sustainable growth, enabling teams to excel, and ensuring that an organization thrives. However, a dangerous trend has infiltrated the corporate world—**manipulation** disguised as management. While this approach may create an illusion of success in the short term, its long-term repercussions are often devastating.

The Birth of Manipulation

Manipulation in management typically begins subtly, often in the form of data misrepresentation. A manipulated sales report, inflated profitability figures, or skewed performance metrics may appear to present a thriving organization. Yet, this distorted reality misleads stakeholders, erodes trust, and sets the stage for poor decision-making.

Managers and executives may justify such actions as necessary for **meeting targets, securing promotions**, or **attracting investors**. But beneath these justifications lies a fragile foundation that cannot support sustainable growth.

Manipulation in management typically begins subtly. A manager, pressured to meet aggressive targets, may alter a few metrics in a report. Executives eager to please investors might overstate market performance or underreport risks. What starts as minor adjustments can snowball into systemic deception.

For example, **Enron Corporation** was once hailed as an innovative leader in the energy sector. However, behind the scenes, its leaders employed complex accounting tactics to hide debt and inflate profits. The initial success created by these manipulations eventually collapsed, leading to one of the largest corporate bankruptcies in history.

Such practices often emerge from a culture that prioritizes appearances over authenticity. Leaders convince themselves that manipulation is a means to an end—a temporary solution to buy time or secure resources. But the consequences often spiral out of control.

Short-Term Wins, Long-Term Losses

Organizations that rely on manipulated data may experience initial gains—stock prices rise, stakeholders celebrate perceived successes, and leadership basks in temporary glory. However, these "wins" come at a cost:

- **Eroded Credibility**: Once discovered, manipulated data undermines the trust of employees, investors, and customers.
- **Poor Decision-Making**: Wrong data leads to wrong strategies, misaligned goals, and squandered resources.
- **Cultural Decay**: A culture of manipulation breeds toxicity, discourages transparency, and drives talent away.

For instance, the collapse of several high-profile companies serves as a sobering reminder of what happens when leadership prioritizes appearances over authenticity. These cases reveal that no amount of manipulation can shield a business from the consequences of unsound decisions.

Organizations that rely on manipulated data may enjoy immediate benefits:

1. **Investor Confidence Increases**: Artificially high performance metrics attract funding and drive up stock prices.
2. **Recognition for Leadership**: Executives and managers are celebrated for "achieving" results.
3. **Increased Market Share**: Misrepresented capabilities can outpace competition temporarily.

However, these wins come with steep long-term costs:

- **Financial Collapse**: Manipulated financial data often leads to poor strategic decisions, ultimately driving companies into bankruptcy.
- **Reputational Damage**: Customers, investors, and employees lose trust in organizations that prioritize deceit.
- **Legal Repercussions**: Manipulation can result in lawsuits, regulatory fines, and even criminal charges.

Consider the case of **Theranos**, a company that claimed revolutionary advancements in blood testing technology. Founder Elizabeth Holmes misrepresented the capabilities of the company's products, leading to skyrocketing valuations. When the truth emerged, the company collapsed, resulting in criminal charges and billions in losses for investors.

The Ripple Effect on Organizational Culture

The impact of manipulation extends beyond financial metrics—it permeates organizational culture. When manipulation becomes a norm:

1. **Ethics are Compromised**: Employees adopt a **"results at any cost"** mindset, further entrenching unethical practices.
2. **Talent Retention Plummets**: Top performers leave environments where dishonesty prevails, taking their skills to competitors.
3. **Innovation Stalls**: Creativity and problem-solving suffer in a culture that prioritizes deception over progress.

When manipulation infiltrates management, its impact goes beyond financial statements:

1. **Eroded Trust**: Employees lose confidence in leadership, leading to disengagement and turnover.
2. **Perpetuated Unethical Behaviour**: Once manipulation is normalized, it spreads across departments, affecting everything from hiring practices to customer interactions.

3. **Reduced Morale**: Talented employees, demotivated by toxic work environments, either underperform or leave.

For instance, organizations with high turnover rates often find themselves in a vicious cycle: the cost of replacing talent escalates, while the remaining workforce struggles with increased workloads and diminished morale. This toxic culture drives even more employees to leave.

Breaking the Cycle

To break free from the illusion of success through manipulation, organizations must:

- **Embrace Transparency**: Leaders should commit to honest reporting and data-driven decisions, even when the truth is uncomfortable.
  - Adopt **open-book management practices**, sharing accurate data with employees and stakeholders.
  - **Regularly audit internal processes** to ensure compliance and accuracy.
- **Foster Accountability**: Establish mechanisms to ensure that manipulation is identified and addressed promptly.
  - **Create whistleblower protection programs** to encourage reporting of unethical practices.
  - **Institute robust checks** and balances for **data reporting**.
- **Promote Ethical Leadership**: Train leaders to prioritize integrity, focusing on long-term goals rather than short-term optics.
  - **Train leaders** to prioritize ethics over expediency.
  - **Establish clear consequences for unethical behaviour** at all levels of the organization.

Case in Point

Consider the rise and fall of organizations that became synonymous with corporate scandal due to manipulated data. Their stories illustrate how manipulation might provide a temporary boost, but the eventual fallout damages reputations, careers, and entire industries.

Case Studies in Contrast: Success Without Manipulation

While manipulation can lead to disaster, organizations that prioritize integrity achieve sustainable success.

Patagonia, the outdoor clothing company, stands as a beacon of ethical management. By being transparent about its supply chain and committing to sustainable practices, the company has not only built trust with its customers but also achieved long-term profitability.

Similarly, **Unilever's Sustainable Living Plan** emphasizes honest reporting and responsible leadership. By embedding ethics into its business model, the company has gained market share while reducing environmental impact.

The True Measure of Success

Success is not measured by manipulated metrics but by authentic progress. It is about building resilient organizations that can withstand scrutiny and thrive in a competitive landscape. Leaders who prioritize ethics over expediency will not only achieve sustainable success but also inspire their teams to do the same.

True success in management is not measured by manipulated metrics but by authentic progress. Organizations must strive for:

- **Sustainability**: Building systems that withstand scrutiny and adapt to future challenges.

- **Resilience**: Cultivating a culture that thrives on transparency and innovation.

- **Trust**: Ensuring that stakeholders—employees, customers, and investors—feel confident in the organization's integrity.

The illusion of success through manipulation is tempting but fleeting. Leaders who embrace ethics and transparency will create legacies that outlast their tenure, inspiring teams and building organizations that stand the test of time.

The Birth of Manipulation in Diverse Industries

Manipulation in management is not industry-specific; it manifests uniquely in different sectors. Regardless of the context, the core issue remains the same—short-term gains through unethical practices often result in long-term instability. Below, we explore how manipulation manifests across industries.

1. Banking, Financial Services, and Insurance (BFSI)

The BFSI sector is often under scrutiny because of its critical role in the global economy. Manipulation in this sector frequently revolves around misrepresenting financial performance, risk profiles, or compliance with regulations.

- **Case Study: 2008 Financial Crisis**

  Financial institutions like Lehman Brothers manipulated their risk exposure, inflating the perceived health of their portfolios. Complex financial instruments, such as subprime mortgage-backed securities, were sold to unsuspecting investors. When the truth surfaced, it triggered a global financial meltdown, leading to massive job losses and economic hardship.

- **Long-Term Impact**

  Manipulating data erodes trust in the financial system. Institutions that survived the crisis, like JPMorgan Chase, rebuilt credibility by emphasizing risk management and transparency.

Breaking the Cycle:

- Establish robust compliance systems.
- Foster a culture of accountability with regular external audits.

2. Consulting Firms

Consulting firms, known for advising businesses, often face pressure to deliver results to clients, which can lead to manipulation of reports and benchmarks.

- **Scenario: Inflated ROI Predictions**

    A consulting firm promises a client a 40% ROI through a digital transformation project. To align with this target, consultants tweak benchmarks, set unrealistic KPIs, and underreport challenges. While the client initially celebrates, project inefficiencies and overruns soon become apparent.

- **Long-Term Impact**

    Such practices damage the consulting firm's reputation, making it difficult to secure future contracts. In contrast, firms like McKinsey thrive because of their commitment to transparency and realistic goal setting.

Breaking the Cycle:

- Use industry-standard benchmarking tools.
- Prioritize ethical client management practices.

---

3. Plant/Factory Organizations: Pharma, Automobile, Steel, Cement

Manipulation in manufacturing and heavy industries often involves cutting corners in production, falsifying compliance reports, or inflating output figures.

- **Case Study: Volkswagen Emissions Scandal**

    In 2015, Volkswagen was found to have installed software in diesel engines to cheat on emissions tests. The manipulation allowed vehicles to pass regulatory tests while emitting pollutants far beyond permissible limits. The company faced billions in fines and a massive reputational blow.

- **Scenario: Safety Data in Pharma**

    In the pharmaceutical industry, some companies have been accused of suppressing unfavourable clinical trial data to expedite drug approvals. While this ensures faster time-to-market, the health risks for consumers can be catastrophic.

- **Long-Term Impact**

    - Loss of consumer trust and market share.
    - Hefty regulatory fines and legal liabilities.

Breaking the Cycle:

- Build a compliance-first culture.
- Invest in transparent supply chain and production audits.

---

4. Dealers and Distributors

Manipulation in dealer and distributor networks often involves inventory hoarding, false sales reporting, or offering unauthorized discounts to meet targets.

- **Scenario: Automobile Dealers**

    To meet sales targets, dealers report "phantom sales" by registering vehicles in bulk under fictitious customers. While this inflates short-term sales figures, it creates logistical issues and financial strain when the vehicles remain unsold.

- **Long-Term Impact**

    - Damage to brand reputation.
    - Strained relationships with manufacturers.

Breaking the Cycle:

- Real-time monitoring of inventory and sales.

- Incentivize honest reporting over inflated numbers.

---

5. Start-ups

Start-ups often operate in high-pressure environments where securing funding or gaining market share is critical. This pressure can lead to exaggerated user metrics, revenue projections, or product capabilities.

- **Case Study: WeWork**

    WeWork presented itself as a high-growth start-up, inflating occupancy rates and overestimating market potential. These manipulations led to a failed IPO and significant investor losses.

- **Scenario: Fake Customer Reviews in Tech Start-ups**

    Start-ups in the tech space may fabricate user reviews or exaggerate product capabilities to gain traction. While this might attract early adopters, poor customer experiences can tarnish the company's reputation.

- **Long-Term Impact**

    - Loss of investor confidence.
    - Reduced market competitiveness.

Breaking the Cycle:

- Establish clear governance frameworks.
- Focus on sustainable growth metrics.

Industry-Wide Commonalities

Despite sectoral differences, the underlying patterns of manipulation are similar:

1. **Pressure to Perform**: Organizations often prioritize short-term gains over sustainable practices.
2. **Lack of Oversight**: Weak internal controls enable unethical practices.
3. **Inadequate Training**: Leadership lacks the skills to manage complex, ethical decision-making.

Solutions for Industry-Specific Challenges

1. BFSI:

Implement AI-driven risk assessment tools to reduce human intervention in decision-making.

Implement AI-Driven Risk Assessment Tools

In the Banking, Financial Services, and Insurance (BFSI) sector, manual intervention in risk assessment often leads to errors, biases, and manipulation of data. AI-driven risk assessment tools offer a robust alternative, automating complex processes and ensuring accuracy, consistency, and integrity.

How AI-Driven Risk Assessment Works:

- **Data Aggregation and Analysis:**

  AI systems process vast amounts of structured and unstructured data from multiple sources, including customer transactions, credit history, market trends, and economic indicators.

- **Predictive Modelling:**

    AI uses machine learning algorithms to predict potential risks, such as credit defaults, fraud, or market fluctuations. For example, banks use AI to forecast customer creditworthiness or identify fraudulent transactions.

- **Real-Time Monitoring:**

    AI tools provide continuous monitoring, enabling institutions to identify and address risks as they arise rather than relying on retrospective analyses.

Advantages of AI in Risk Assessment:

- **Bias Reduction:** Eliminates human biases in decision-making, such as favouritism in loan approvals.
- **Enhanced Accuracy:** Provides precise risk evaluations based on comprehensive datasets.
- **Cost Efficiency:** Reduces the need for large teams of analysts, lowering operational costs.
- **Scalability:** Capable of handling large volumes of data as organizations grow.

Case Study: JP Morgan Chase

JP Morgan Chase has implemented AI in credit risk assessment and fraud detection. Their COiN (Contract Intelligence) program uses AI to review legal documents, identifying risks and compliance issues with high accuracy and speed. This approach has significantly improved operational efficiency and decision-making integrity.

Best Practices for Implementation:

1. **Choose the Right Technology Partners:** Partner with reliable AI vendors or build in-house capabilities.
2. **Ensure Data Quality:** The effectiveness of AI tools relies heavily on the quality and diversity of the input data.

3. **Ethical AI Deployment:** Incorporate fairness and transparency to avoid unintended biases in AI models.
4. **Training and Adaptation:** Train staff to work alongside AI tools for optimal integration and outcomes.

Conduct regular stress tests to ensure resilience.

Stress tests are critical for ensuring the stability of financial institutions, especially during economic or market downturns. These tests simulate adverse scenarios to evaluate the organization's ability to withstand shocks and maintain operations.

What Are Stress Tests?

Stress tests involve hypothetical scenarios such as:

- **Economic Recession:** Sharp declines in GDP and rising unemployment rates.
- **Market Volatility:** Sudden drops in stock or bond markets.
- **Credit Crises:** Mass loan defaults or corporate bankruptcies.

Benefits of Stress Testing:

- **Risk Identification:** Uncover vulnerabilities in capital reserves, credit portfolios, or operational capabilities.
- **Preparedness:** Enables organizations to develop contingency plans for potential crises.
- **Regulatory Compliance:** Many countries mandate stress tests as part of their financial regulations.

Case Study: European Banking Authority (EBA)

The EBA conducts annual stress tests for major European banks. The 2021 stress test simulated a severe economic downturn, evaluating banks' capital adequacy under adverse conditions. The results highlighted institutions that needed to improve their risk buffers, leading to corrective measures before a real crisis could occur.

Steps for Conducting Stress Tests:

1. **Scenario Design:** Develop realistic adverse scenarios based on historical data and emerging risks.
2. **Model Development:** Use statistical and econometric models to simulate the impact of these scenarios.
3. **Analysis and Reporting:** Evaluate the results and identify areas of vulnerability. Share findings with stakeholders, including regulators and investors.
4. **Corrective Action Plans:** Implement measures to address identified risks, such as increasing capital reserves or revising investment strategies.

Integration of AI and Stress Testing

When combined, AI and stress testing form a powerful framework for risk management in BFSI:

- **AI-Powered Scenarios:** AI can analyze macroeconomic data to create more dynamic and accurate stress scenarios.
- **Real-Time Adjustments:** AI enables financial institutions to adapt stress tests based on real-time market conditions.
- **Enhanced Insights:** By integrating AI analytics, institutions can identify deeper trends and correlations that manual methods might overlook.

Conclusion

Implementing AI-driven risk assessment tools and conducting regular stress tests are indispensable for building resilience in the BFSI sector. Together, they create a proactive risk management approach that not only protects against manipulation but also ensures the long-term stability and trustworthiness of financial institutions.

2. **Consulting Firms**:
   - ➢ Provide clients with evidence-based insights supported by robust data analysis.
   - ➢ Conduct internal audits of client deliverables.

3. **Manufacturing**:
   - ➢ Use IoT and blockchain for transparent production tracking.
   - ➢ Incentivize sustainable practices over output quantity.

4. **Dealers and Distributors**:
   - ➢ Align incentives with customer satisfaction metrics, not just sales targets.
   - ➢ Digitize sales reporting for accuracy.

5. **Start-ups**:
   - ➢ Partner with ethical investors who prioritize long-term growth.
   - ➢ Focus on user retention over acquisition as a key performance metric.

Conclusion: Building a Culture of Integrity Across Industries

The illusion of success through manipulation might appear as a tempting shortcut, but it erodes the very foundation of businesses. Industries that embrace transparency, prioritize ethical leadership, and commit to sustainable practices are the ones that ultimately thrive.

Understanding manipulation in management

Manipulation in management occurs when individuals or groups deliberately alter facts, perceptions, or outcomes to gain personal or organizational advantage, often at the expense of transparency, ethics, and long-term sustainability. This practice, while sometimes disguised as strategic management, can have profoundly negative consequences for the organization, its employees, and its stakeholders.

1. The Roots of Manipulation in Management

- **Incentive Misalignment:**

  Misaligned KPIs or performance metrics often drive managers to manipulate data to meet short-term goals rather than focusing on sustainable growth.

  o Example: Sales managers inflating revenue projections to meet quarterly targets.

- **Pressure from Leadership:**

  Unrealistic expectations from top executives or shareholders can compel middle and senior management to distort reality.

  o Example: Artificially enhancing financial statements to meet investor demands.

- **Cultural Norms:**

  n some organizations, manipulation becomes ingrained as part of the corporate culture, often under the guise of "being resourceful."

---

2. Forms of Manipulation in Management

- **Data Manipulation:**

  Altering or fabricating reports, financial statements, or analytics to present a more favourable picture.

  o Example: Adjusting expense reports to show reduced costs while actual inefficiencies persist.

- **Information Withholding:**

  Selectively sharing information to influence decisions or gain leverage.

- o   Example: Withholding data about a product's performance issues during board discussions.

- **Emotional Manipulation:**
- Using fear, guilt, or favouritism to control employees or stakeholders.

    - o   Example: Threatening job security to push employees into unethical practices.

- **Nepotism and Bias:**

    Favouring certain individuals or teams based on personal relationships rather than merit.

3. Why Manipulation is Detrimental

- **Short-Term Gains, Long-Term Losses:**

    Manipulation might yield immediate results but undermines trust, morale, and the organization's reputation over time.

- **Toxic Work Culture:**

    Employees who witness manipulation may lose faith in leadership, resulting in higher turnover and decreased engagement.

- **Erosion of Trust:**

    Manipulation damages relationships with stakeholders, including employees, customers, and investors.

- **Operational Inefficiencies:**

    Decisions based on manipulated data often lead to resource misallocation and strategic missteps.

4. Real-World Examples of Management Manipulation

- **Enron Scandal:**

Enron's leadership manipulated financial statements to inflate earnings and hide debt, leading to one of the largest corporate collapses in history.

The Enron Scandal, one of the most infamous cases of corporate fraud, unfolded in the early 2000s when the energy giant was found guilty of extensive financial manipulation. Enron's leadership used complex accounting practices, such as off-balance-sheet entities, to hide debt and inflate earnings, creating an illusion of robust financial health. These fraudulent activities misled investors and regulators, resulting in a stock price surge that masked the company's unstable foundation. When the truth surfaced, Enron declared bankruptcy in 2001, erasing $74 billion in shareholder value, devastating employee pensions, and leading to the dissolution of Arthur Andersen, one of the largest auditing firms at the time. The scandal profoundly impacted corporate governance, leading to the creation of the Sarbanes-Oxley Act to enhance transparency and accountability.

- **Volkswagen Emissions Scandal:**

Manipulating emissions data to meet regulatory standards caused severe reputational damage and billions in fines.

The Volkswagen Emissions Scandal, often referred to as **"Dieselgate,"** emerged in 2015 when the company was found to have installed software in millions of diesel vehicles to cheat emissions tests. This software enabled cars to meet regulatory standards during testing but emitted nitrogen oxide levels up to 40 times the legal limit during real-world driving conditions. The manipulation, aimed at maintaining market share and regulatory compliance, led to significant reputational damage, a global recall of affected vehicles, and over $30 billion in fines, settlements, and legal costs. The scandal highlighted the long-term consequences of unethical practices and shook consumer trust in the brand.

- **Startup Overvaluations:**

Many startups, under pressure to attract investors, manipulate financial projections, leading to unsustainable business models.

Startup overvaluations often stem from inflated financial projections designed to attract investors, creating a facade of rapid growth and profitability. One notable example is **WeWork**, which faced scrutiny in 2019 during its attempt to go public. The company, initially valued at $47 billion, was revealed to have exaggerated revenue potential while downplaying operational losses. Leadership's focus on expansion at the expense of sustainable business practices resulted in plummeting valuations and the eventual resignation of its CEO. The debacle highlighted how overestimating market readiness and manipulating projections can lead to investor mistrust and significant setbacks for startups, emphasizing the importance of transparency and realistic goal setting.

5. The Psychology Behind Manipulation

- **Fear of Failure:**

    Managers often manipulate to avoid consequences of underperformance or failure.

- **Desire for Power:**

    Manipulation can be a tool to consolidate authority or influence within an organization.

- **Insecurity:**
    A lack of confidence in one's abilities or decisions may drive individuals to manipulate outcomes.

6. Identifying Signs of Manipulation

- **Inconsistent Data:**

    Frequent discrepancies between reported and actual performance metrics.

- **Closed Communication Loops:**

    Leaders or teams controlling the flow of information to maintain influence.

- **Lack of Accountability:**

    A culture where results are prioritized over ethical processes.

---

7. How to Combat Manipulation in Management

- **Promote Transparency:**

    Encourage open reporting systems and cross-functional collaboration to reduce opportunities for manipulation.

- **Conduct Regular Audits:**

    Regular internal audits and organizational culture assessments can identify manipulative practices early.

- **Set Clear Ethical Standards:**

    Establish a code of ethics and enforce it consistently across all levels of the organization.

- **Leverage Technology:**

    Use AI and analytics tools to monitor patterns and anomalies in data that may indicate manipulation.

- **Strengthen Leadership Training:**

    Train leaders to prioritize ethical decision-making and align their goals with long-term organizational sustainability.

8. The Role of HR in Addressing Manipulation

- **Organizational Culture Audits:**

    HR can use surveys, interviews, and analytics to assess the cultural health of the organization and identify areas prone to manipulation.

Organizational culture audits are critical tools for HR to evaluate the underlying **Core values practices** in actual business situations, behaviours, and dynamics that shape an **organization's work environment**.

By leveraging surveys, interviews, and data analytics, HR can uncover areas where manipulation, favouritism, or unethical practices may be taking root.

For instance, anonymous employee feedback surveys can highlight concerns about transparency or trust in leadership, while analytics can identify patterns of high turnover in specific departments.

Interviews with employees and managers can provide deeper insights into systemic issues or potential conflicts.

A well-conducted **Organisation culture audit** not only identifies problem areas but also offers actionable recommendations to foster a healthier, more ethical, and more productive workplace.

Organizational culture audits are critical tools HR can use to evaluate the health of workplace culture and uncover vulnerabilities such as manipulation or unethical practices.

For example, a multinational tech firm faced high employee turnover and declining engagement scores, prompting an HR-led culture audit.

The audit included **anonymous surveys** to gather employee perceptions, **structured interviews** with key personnel to understand leadership dynamics, and **data analytics** to identify trends in attrition and performance metrics.

Key components of the audit revealed inconsistencies in performance appraisals and favouritism in promotions. These findings led to actionable recommendations, such as implementing unbiased evaluation systems, leadership training, and improved communication channels. The audit not only restored trust but also enhanced organizational alignment and morale.

- **Competency Frameworks:**

    Clearly defined competency standards for all roles can ensure fair recruitment and promotion practices.

The number of competencies required for different levels within an organization can vary based on the role's complexity and scope of responsibility. However, we can provide general guidelines:

1. Base Level Employee:

- **Minimum Number of Competencies**: Typically, a base level employee should have between **4 to 6 competencies**. These competencies should focus on essential skills such as communication, teamwork, problem-solving, adaptability, and technical proficiency. These competencies are sufficient for effective job performance at the operational level.

2. Leadership CXO Team:

- **Maximum Number of Competencies**: The leadership team, including Chief Executive Officers (CXOs), should possess between **10 to 15 competencies**. These competencies are more complex and strategic in nature, encompassing not only technical skills but also leadership, strategic thinking, decision-making, financial acumen, stakeholder engagement, and vision setting. This broader range ensures they can guide the organization through complex challenges, maintain alignment with the business strategy, and drive sustainable growth.

By clearly defining these competencies and assessing employees' alignment with them, organizations can ensure they have the right people in the right roles, ready to meet current and future challenges.

- **Employee Feedback Mechanisms:**

    Encourage employees to report unethical practices through anonymous channels without fear of retaliation.

Example: The Boeing Case Study – Promoting Ethical Reporting through Employee Feedback Mechanisms

Background: In the wake of several operational failures, including the 737 Max crisis, Boeing faced severe scrutiny over safety and ethical practices. A key issue was that employees felt discouraged from reporting safety concerns due to fear of retaliation or career repercussions. To address this, Boeing implemented robust employee feedback mechanisms aimed at encouraging whistleblowing and ensuring a culture of transparency.

Key Components:

1. **Anonymous Reporting Channels**: Boeing introduced confidential hotlines and online portals where employees could anonymously report concerns related to safety, ethics, and compliance. These channels were promoted widely across the organization, emphasizing non-retaliation guarantees.

2. **Employee Surveys and Regular Check-ins**: Regular surveys and one-on-one meetings were conducted to gauge the cultural health and to understand if employees felt comfortable reporting unethical practices. The results were used to assess employee concerns and to make necessary changes to company policies and procedures.

3. **Follow-Up and Response Mechanisms**: Boeing set up a dedicated team to review reports and investigate concerns. Responses were communicated transparently, showing that management took employee feedback seriously and acted upon it. Additionally, regular updates and feedback on issues and resolutions were shared with employees to build trust in the system.

Profitable Outcome: By fostering an environment where employees felt safe to report unethical behaviour, Boeing was able to identify critical safety concerns before they became major crises. This not only restored trust among employees but also bolstered the company's reputation and brand. The proactive feedback mechanism allowed Boeing to implement changes swiftly, addressing systemic issues and preventing future incidents. In the long run, this approach contributed to reducing operational risks, improving employee morale, and stabilizing the organization financially.

This example underscores the importance of robust employee feedback mechanisms in maintaining ethical standards, fostering a positive organizational culture, and achieving sustainable success.

Conclusion

Manipulation in management is a symptom of deeper systemic issues. Addressing it requires a comprehensive approach that combines ethical leadership, robust systems, and a culture of transparency. By recognizing and eliminating manipulative practices, organizations can build trust, improve morale, and achieve sustainable success.

How data forging starts the chain of bad decisions

Data forging, or manipulating data to present a misleading picture, can have far-reaching consequences, often leading to a series of bad decisions that can cripple an organization. This practice distorts reality and can affect strategic planning, financial performance, risk management, and overall decision-making processes. Here's a detailed look at how data forging can start this chain reaction and examples from real cases.

Example: The Enron Scandal

- **Chain of Bad Decisions**: In the case of Enron, the leadership manipulated financial statements using complex accounting tricks, such as Special Purpose Entities (SPEs), to hide debt and inflate earnings. The data presented was crafted to show a picture of profitability and growth, masking the company's precarious financial health. This manipulation led to a series of misguided strategic decisions, including aggressive expansion and acquisition strategies based on unrealistic financial projections.

- **Impact**: The deception not only misled investors and analysts but also led to the company's eventual bankruptcy in 2001. The failure of Enron wiped out $74 billion in shareholder value, put 20,600 employees out of work, and caused a ripple effect across the global financial markets. The scandal also resulted in changes to corporate governance regulations, such as the Sarbanes-Oxley Act, to curb such practices.

Case Study: Volkswagen Emissions Scandal

- **Chain of Bad Decisions**: Volkswagen manipulated emissions tests by installing software that detected when a car was being tested and adjusted the emission controls accordingly. This manipulation was done to meet regulatory standards in key markets like the United States, despite their real-world emissions being far above acceptable limits.

- **Bad Decisions Resulting from Data Forging**:
    - **Marketing Strategies**: The falsified emissions data allowed Volkswagen to market its vehicles as environmentally friendly, attracting customers with the promise of low emissions. This misled consumers and created a competitive advantage based on false information.
    - **Expansion Strategies**: Volkswagen's management made decisions to expand production and sales based on inflated profitability forecasts, leading to unsustainable growth. The manipulated data led to overestimates of market share and underestimated operational costs.

- **Impact**: The emissions scandal resulted in significant financial losses, including a recall of 11 million vehicles, fines totalling over $30 billion, and a severe drop in stock value. The reputational damage was extensive, undermining consumer trust and prompting regulatory investigations worldwide.

Data and Statistics:

1. **Enron**: At its peak, Enron was valued at $74 billion, but when the truth about the accounting fraud was revealed, the company declared bankruptcy, and investors lost billions. It's estimated that employees lost $1.2 billion in pension savings due to the company's collapse.

2. **Volkswagen**: Volkswagen's emissions scandal led to fines, penalties, and costs totalling over $30 billion. The company faced legal battles in multiple countries and saw a 30% drop in market value after the scandal was disclosed.

3. **Statistical Impact of Data Forging**:
    - **Long-term Financial Damage**: Data manipulation often leads to poor decision-making based on inaccurate financial models. Research has shown that companies involved in data manipulation face a significant drop in stock prices (an average drop of 20-30%) and long-term underperformance compared to their industry peers.
    - **Reputational Damage**: A study published in the Harvard Business Review found that companies with a history of data manipulation face longer recovery periods and higher costs associated with reputation damage and loss of customer trust.

Data forging not only distorts the immediate business environment but also sets in motion a chain of bad decisions that affect all levels of the organization—from strategic planning to operational decisions. It's a practice that can cripple long-term sustainability and profitability, demonstrating the critical need for transparency and integrity in data management and decision-making processes.

Case studies: Organizations that suffered due to manipulated analytics

Here are three corporate case studies illustrating how organizations suffered due to manipulated analytics:

1. Enron Scandal

Background: Enron, once one of the largest energy companies in the United States, engaged in accounting fraud to artificially inflate its financial performance. The company used off-balance-sheet entities and other complex financial instruments to hide debt and overstate profits. This manipulation allowed Enron to present a façade of strong financial health and market leadership.

Impact: The manipulated financial data led to a false sense of security for investors, regulators, and employees. When the fraud was discovered in 2001, Enron's stock price plummeted from $90 to less than $1, causing shareholders to lose approximately $74 billion in value. The collapse resulted in the bankruptcy of Enron, loss of 20,600 jobs, and a significant reputational hit to the company. The scandal also spurred regulatory changes, such as the Sarbanes-Oxley Act, to prevent such fraudulent practices in the future.

2. Volkswagen Emissions Scandal

Background: Volkswagen was found to have manipulated emissions data in millions of diesel cars using software designed to detect when a vehicle was being tested and adjust performance accordingly. This allowed the vehicles to pass emissions tests but emit pollutants at far higher levels under real-world driving conditions.

Impact: The manipulation misled regulators, customers, and investors about the environmental performance of their vehicles. When the truth surfaced in 2015, Volkswagen faced significant backlash, including $30 billion in fines, settlements, and recall costs. The company's reputation was severely damaged, affecting its brand image and customer loyalty. Sales dropped significantly, and the company was forced to spend heavily on corrective measures, such as vehicle recalls and software updates. The scandal also led to legal actions in multiple countries and a drop in stock value.

3. Theranos

Background: Theranos, a blood-testing startup, falsely claimed its technology could perform a range of diagnostic tests with just a few drops of blood. However, it was later revealed that the company manipulated data to overstate the accuracy and capability of its tests.

Impact: The manipulation of analytics allowed Theranos to attract high-profile investors and enter partnerships with major healthcare companies. When the fraud was exposed in 2015, it resulted in significant legal and financial repercussions for the company's executives, including its founder, Elizabeth Holmes. The organization's valuation, which once peaked at $9 billion, collapsed, and it was dissolved. Investors lost millions, and the scandal tarnished the reputations of key figures involved. The case also prompted increased scrutiny of biotech startups and their claims, emphasizing the need for transparency and accuracy in health-related data.

These case studies demonstrate how the manipulation of analytics can lead to severe consequences, from financial losses and legal penalties to reputational damage and the eventual downfall of once-prominent organizations.

Chapter 2: Ethics and Accountability in Decision-Making

Why ethics matter in management practices

The ripple effect of unethical practices on organizational culture

Developing accountability frameworks to prevent manipulation

Ethics and Accountability in Decision-Making

Ethics and Accountability in Decision-Making - Why it Matters for Shareholders

For shareholders, ethics and accountability in decision-making are crucial because they directly influence the financial health and long-term sustainability of the company. Transparent, ethical decision-making builds trust with investors, ensuring that their investments are secure and that the company is operating in the best interest of its shareholders. When leaders make ethical decisions, they avoid deceptive practices such as data manipulation, which can lead to financial misreporting, loss of value, and legal repercussions. This transparency fosters investor confidence and can lead to higher stock prices, stable returns, and sustained growth. Shareholders benefit from a stable organization with strong governance practices, protecting their investment against risks such as market volatility and corporate scandals.

Ethics and Accountability in Decision-Making - Why it Matters for Employees

For employees, ethical decision-making in leadership sets the tone for workplace culture and employee morale. When leaders make decisions based on integrity, it fosters a sense of trust and respect within the organization. Employees feel valued and are more likely to stay loyal to the company, contributing to a positive workplace environment and reducing turnover. Ethical behaviour also promotes a fair work environment, where employees feel confident in reporting unethical practices without fear of retaliation. This can lead to higher employee engagement, productivity, and satisfaction, which are directly linked to the company's overall performance. Ethical leadership ensures that the well-being of employees is a priority, creating a **supportive work environment** that aligns with the **company's values and goals.**

Ethics and Accountability in Decision-Making - Why it Matters for Customers

For customers, ethics and accountability translate into trust and reliability in the products and services they purchase. When companies are transparent in their practices, customers are more likely to trust the quality, safety, and sustainability of the products. Ethical decision-making ensures that the company is not cutting corners or engaging in misleading practices, which can lead to harm to consumers. For example, companies that manipulate product safety data can put customers at risk, damaging their health and well-being. By maintaining high ethical standards, companies build a reputation for honesty and responsibility, which can lead to customer loyalty and a competitive edge in the market.

Ethics and Accountability in Decision-Making - Why it Matters for Vendors

For vendors and suppliers, ethical decision-making by a company is crucial for maintaining long-term business relationships. Vendors rely on companies to be transparent in their supply chain practices, including fair payment, sustainability, and adherence to environmental and social standards. When a company manipulates data or behaves unethically, it can disrupt the entire supply chain, affecting the livelihood of vendors and suppliers. Ethical decision-making ensures that vendors are treated fairly, paid promptly, and not subjected to unfair practices, such as low-balling or supply chain disruptions. This creates a stable and mutually beneficial relationship, allowing vendors to plan their operations effectively and ensuring the supply chain remains resilient and sustainable.

Ethics and Accountability in Decision-Making - Why it Matters for Environment & Society

For the environment and society, ethical decision-making in business is essential for sustainable development. Companies that engage in data manipulation, environmental degradation, or disregard social responsibility can have a negative impact on the planet and communities. They may ignore the environmental footprint of their operations, fail to comply with regulations, or avoid investing in sustainable practices like recycling or waste management. Ethical decision-making ensures that businesses take responsibility for their impact, adopting practices that reduce harm to the environment and contribute to social well-being. This includes initiatives such as reducing greenhouse gas emissions, conserving water, using renewable energy, and supporting community development. By prioritizing ethics and accountability, companies can create a positive legacy for future generations and contribute to global sustainability goals.

Why ethics matter in management practices

Ethics in management practices are crucial because they shape the culture and reputation of an organization, influencing relationships with shareholders, employees, customers, vendors, and society at large. Ethical management practices ensure transparency, accountability, and fairness in decision-making, which in turn fosters trust and builds long-term value for all stakeholders. When managers prioritize ethics, they prevent behaviours such as data manipulation, conflicts of interest, and deceptive marketing practices that can lead to financial misreporting, legal liabilities, and reputational damage. Ethics in management also promote a positive work environment where employees feel valued and motivated, leading to higher engagement and productivity. Furthermore, ethical practices are essential for maintaining compliance with regulatory standards, which protects the company from legal risks and ensures its operations are sustainable.

Three Best Ethical Companies in the World

1.Patagonia:

Known for its commitment to environmental sustainability and ethical labour practices, Patagonia is a pioneer in corporate responsibility. The company's dedication to reducing its carbon footprint, using sustainable materials, and supporting environmental causes sets it apart. Patagonia's management practices emphasize transparency and accountability, allowing stakeholders to understand its sustainability efforts and the impact of its business decisions on the environment. The company also encourages employees to spend 16 hours per month working on environmental activism, promoting a culture of ethics and responsibility beyond the corporate realm.

2. Unilever:

Unilever is widely recognized for its focus on sustainable development and ethical practices in management. The company's Sustainable Living Plan guides its operations, aiming to decouple growth from environmental impact. Unilever prioritizes responsible sourcing, reducing waste and water use, and creating products that benefit both consumers and the environment. Its leadership is committed to transparent reporting, engaging with stakeholders on ethical issues, and ensuring that business decisions align with the company's values. Unilever's efforts to maintain ethical management practices have helped it build trust with consumers and investors, leading to sustained growth and resilience in the market.

3. Danone:

Danone is another example of a company that integrates ethical practices into its management framework. The company's B-Corp certification reflects its commitment to environmental and social responsibility, particularly in terms of sustainable sourcing, community impact, and health-focused product offerings. Danone's management practices emphasize transparency, particularly regarding its environmental impact and social initiatives. The company's leadership has made a public commitment to human rights, ethical sourcing, and fair treatment of employees, which has helped it maintain high levels of customer loyalty and a positive reputation in the market.

Ethics matter in management practices because they drive long-term success by fostering trust, accountability, and sustainability across all aspects of the business. These best-in-class companies demonstrate how integrating ethical principles into management decisions can enhance reputation, profitability, and employee satisfaction while contributing positively to society and the environment.

The ripple effect of unethical practices on Organizational Culture

The ripple effect of unethical practices on organizational culture can be profound, leading to severe consequences such as loss of reputation, market share, investor confidence, and ultimately, even business closure. Below, we explore this impact with detailed examples, case studies, statistics, and data.

Ripple Effect of Unethical Practices on Organizational Culture

1. **Loss of Reputation**:

Unethical practices can quickly erode an organization's reputation, leading to a loss of trust among stakeholders including employees, customers, investors, and the public. When companies engage in deceptive practices such as financial misreporting, misleading marketing, or environmental violations, it becomes widely known and affects not only the immediate reputation of the company but also the broader industry. For instance, the global retailer Walmart faced widespread criticism for its unethical labour practices, including gender discrimination and poor treatment of workers in its supply chain. This tarnished its reputation, leading to decreased customer trust and reduced brand loyalty, impacting sales and market share.

2. **Case Study - Wells Fargo**

Background: Wells Fargo, one of the largest banks in the United States, engaged in widespread unethical practices involving the creation of millions of unauthorized customer accounts. Employees were pressured to meet sales targets and quotas, leading them to open accounts without customers' consent to meet performance goals.

Impact: The scandal led to severe financial repercussions, including the firing of over 5,000 employees, the resignation of top executives, and the payment of $2.9 billion in fines and refunds to customers. The company also faced a significant drop in share price, losing more than $22 billion in market value in just a few days after the scandal was revealed. The fallout resulted in the loss of investor confidence, damage to its reputation as a trusted financial institution, and a loss of customers who left for competitors with more transparent practices.

3. **Case Study - Toshiba Scandal**

Background: Toshiba Corporation's management was involved in accounting fraud to inflate profits by over $1.2 billion between 2008 and 2015. Executives manipulated financial data and withheld information from auditors to hide losses and present a falsely optimistic view of the company's financial health.

Impact: The scandal led to a collapse in investor confidence, a dramatic decline in share price, and the loss of key customers and contracts. Toshiba's stock price fell by over 50% after the scandal became public, causing a loss of market value amounting to billions of dollars. The company's reputation was severely damaged, prompting a loss of business in its key markets, including nuclear power and semiconductor sectors. The scandal also led to leadership changes, as the CEO and several top executives resigned. In response, Toshiba embarked on a major restructuring plan, which involved selling non-core assets and shrinking its workforce to restore credibility.

4. **Case Study - Boeing 737 Max Crisis**

Background: The Boeing 737 Max aircraft crisis was triggered by the company's failure to disclose issues with its automated flight control systems. The aircraft was involved in two fatal crashes within five months, leading to the grounding of all 737 Max planes worldwide.

Impact: The unethical practices involved in regulatory reporting and product safety were directly linked to poor communication and oversight. The crisis caused a significant loss of market share for Boeing, a fall in share prices, and a drop in investor confidence. Boeing's stock price fell by nearly 30% following the second crash, representing a loss of $25 billion in market value. The company faced lawsuits from families of victims, airlines, and shareholders, demanding compensation for financial losses and damages.

The crisis prompted Boeing to conduct a comprehensive review of its safety practices, invest heavily in public relations, and undergo significant changes to its management structure and culture to prevent future ethical lapses.

Statistics and Data

- **Wells Fargo**: After the scandal, Wells Fargo's stock dropped by 7%, causing a loss of $22 billion in market value. The company paid $2.9 billion in fines and refunds to affected customers.
- **Toshiba**: Toshiba's stock fell by over 50%, leading to a loss of billions in market value. The company's financial health was severely impacted, forcing a major restructuring to recover credibility.
- **Boeing**: After the 737 Max crisis, Boeing's stock dropped by nearly 30%, resulting in a loss of $25 billion in market value. The company faced billions in legal costs and settlements.

The ripple effect of unethical practices can be far-reaching, affecting not only the company involved but also the broader industry. Unethical behaviour undermines trust, disrupts relationships with customers, and leads to financial instability, often resulting in market exits or closures. These case studies highlight the importance of ethics and accountability in management practices to maintain organizational health, protect shareholder value, and ensure long-term sustainability.

Developing accountability frameworks to prevent manipulation

To prevent manipulation and ensure ethical decision-making within organizations, it is crucial to develop robust accountability frameworks. These frameworks serve as guiding principles that promote transparency, integrity, and compliance, ultimately protecting the organization from reputational damage, financial loss, and regulatory penalties. Below, we explore several examples of these frameworks, detailing how they were designed, their impact on business, and the outcomes they achieved.

Examples and Case Studies of Accountability Frameworks

1. **Case Study - The Sarbanes-Oxley Act (SOX) - United States**

Design and Implementation: The Sarbanes-Oxley Act was enacted in 2002 in response to several high-profile corporate scandals, including Enron and WorldCom, where fraudulent financial reporting was rampant. The act was designed to improve corporate governance, internal controls, and transparency in financial reporting. One of the key components of SOX was the requirement for companies to establish an internal control framework to assess the accuracy and completeness of their financial reports. The Act mandated that CEOs and CFOs personally certify that their company's financial statements are accurate, thereby holding executives accountable for any misreporting.

Impact on Business: The implementation of SOX led to a significant increase in corporate transparency and the establishment of robust internal controls. Companies were required to have independent auditors assess the effectiveness of their internal controls and report any deficiencies. This framework improved the quality of financial disclosures and restored investor confidence by reducing the likelihood of financial manipulation. SOX also introduced harsher penalties for executives involved in fraudulent practices, deterring unethical behaviour.

Outcome: The act's impact was immediate; companies that adopted SOX-compliant internal controls saw a decline in financial misreporting. It created a new standard for corporate accountability, making it harder for executives to manipulate data for personal gain. However, compliance with SOX was costly, requiring significant resources for audits and process documentation. Despite these challenges, the overall outcome was positive—reduced corporate fraud, greater accountability, and a more robust business environment.

2. **Case Study - COSO Framework - Enterprise Risk Management (ERM)**

Design and Implementation: The COSO (Committee of Sponsoring Organizations of the Treadway Commission) Framework is a widely recognized model for enterprise risk management. It provides guidelines for organizations to assess and manage risks related to financial reporting, operations, and compliance. The framework includes principles such as governance and culture, risk assessment, control activities, information and communication, and monitoring activities. These principles are designed to ensure that managers understand their responsibilities, make informed decisions, and maintain transparency.

Impact on Business: By implementing the COSO ERM Framework, companies could better identify, assess, and respond to risks, thereby preventing unethical behaviour and manipulation. The framework encourages a holistic view of risk management, integrating it into strategic planning and operational decision-making. It empowers management to establish a culture of accountability by providing clear guidelines on ethical practices and compliance.

Outcome: The adoption of the COSO Framework led to improved decision-making processes within organizations. It facilitated better monitoring of financial and operational controls, reducing the risk of data manipulation and enhancing the accuracy of financial reports. For example, companies like Pfizer and Johnson & Johnson utilized the COSO ERM framework to enhance their internal controls, leading to better regulatory compliance and a stronger reputation for financial integrity. The framework also helped mitigate risks related to executive compensation, conflicts of interest, and inadequate oversight, thereby reducing the incidence of unethical practices.

3. **Case Study - The UK Corporate Governance Code**

Design and Implementation: The UK Corporate Governance Code provides a framework for effective governance practices for listed companies. It emphasizes the importance of transparency, board accountability, and ethical behaviour in managing companies. The code includes principles for board leadership, effectiveness, remuneration, accountability, and relations with shareholders. One of the key elements is the requirement for companies to establish audit committees that provide oversight of financial reporting and internal controls.

Impact on Business: The UK Corporate Governance Code introduced rigorous standards for transparency and accountability, making it more difficult for companies to engage in manipulative practices. By requiring audit committees to review financial reports and assess the adequacy of internal controls, the code helped companies detect and prevent financial fraud. It also emphasized the need for directors to understand their responsibilities regarding risk management and ethical conduct.

Outcome: The implementation of the UK Corporate Governance Code led to improved corporate behaviour and increased investor confidence. Companies that complied with the code saw a reduction in financial misreporting, a decline in market manipulation, and a lower incidence of executive misconduct. For example, companies like Tesco and BP, which had faced past ethical issues, adopted the code's principles, leading to better corporate governance and recovery of investor trust. The code's impact was also seen in improved shareholder engagement, as it required companies to be more transparent in their decision-making processes, fostering greater accountability.

Impact and Outcome

The development and implementation of robust accountability frameworks are crucial in preventing manipulation in management practices. These frameworks provide a structured approach to ensuring that decision-makers are accountable for their actions, thereby reducing the risk of unethical behaviour. They promote transparency, enhance compliance with regulatory standards, and create a culture of integrity within organizations. By adopting these frameworks, businesses can avoid the financial, reputational, and legal consequences associated with manipulation, leading to sustainable and ethical growth. The frameworks also empower stakeholders—shareholders, employees, customers, vendors, and society—to hold organizations accountable for their actions, thereby fostering a responsible business environment.

Chapter 3: Organizational Culture Audits

Role of HR in identifying cultural and operational gaps

Conducting effective culture audits: Tools and techniques

Addressing root causes of toxicity and turnover

Organizational Culture Audits: An In-depth Analysis

Organizational Culture Audits (OCAs) are essential tools used by Human Resources (HR) departments to assess and measure the health and effectiveness of a company's organizational culture. These audits involve a structured evaluation of the company's values, beliefs, practices, and behaviours to identify areas of risk, unethical practices, and potential manipulation. By conducting OCAs, companies can proactively address issues before they lead to financial loss, reputational damage, and employee turnover. Below, we examine examples and case studies that illustrate the impact of Organizational Culture Audits on business outcomes.

Examples and Case Studies

1. **Case Study - Deloitte's Organizational Culture Audit**

Design and Implementation: Deloitte, a global consulting firm, conducted a comprehensive Organizational Culture Audit to assess its workplace environment and identify potential risks. The audit process involved surveys, focus groups, and interviews with employees across all levels of the organization. The aim was to understand how well the company's culture aligned with its values, how employees perceived leadership, and whether there was a prevalence of manipulation or unethical behaviour.

Impact on Business: The audit revealed several areas where employees felt uncomfortable reporting unethical behaviour due to fear of retaliation. Deloitte discovered that certain managers were manipulating performance data to influence bonuses and promotions unfairly. The company's culture was identified as hierarchical and punitive, leading to suppressed dissent and a lack of transparency in decision-making.

Outcome: As a result of the OCA, Deloitte implemented several changes to foster a more open and accountable culture. The audit findings led to the establishment of anonymous reporting channels for employees to voice concerns about unethical practices without fear of reprisal. The company also introduced training programs focused on ethical decision-making and transparency. By addressing these issues, Deloitte improved its organizational culture, reduced employee turnover, and restored trust among stakeholders. The audit not only helped in enhancing internal compliance but also strengthened its reputation as a leader in ethical business practices.

2. **Case Study - Wells Fargo's Organizational Culture Audit**

Design and Implementation: Following a scandal where employees created fake accounts to meet sales targets, Wells Fargo undertook an Organizational Culture Audit to assess its corporate culture. This audit focused on understanding how the aggressive sales culture and performance targets influenced employee behaviour. The process included surveys, interviews, and focus groups with employees at various levels, from frontline staff to senior management.

Impact on Business: The audit revealed that the pressure to meet sales goals led to manipulation of metrics and unethical behaviour among employees. The culture at Wells Fargo was identified as one that promoted short-term success at the expense of long-term integrity. Employees reported feeling pressured to prioritize sales performance over customer service, resulting in a widespread practice of opening unauthorized accounts.

Outcome: The findings from the OCA prompted Wells Fargo to implement a series of corrective measures. These included restructuring the organizational hierarchy to reduce pressures on sales targets, revising performance evaluation systems, and creating more robust compliance and ethics training programs. The audit also led to changes in how performance was measured and rewarded, with a greater emphasis on ethical behaviour and customer satisfaction. The outcome was a significant culture shift at Wells Fargo, restoring employee morale and regaining customer trust.

However, the damage to the company's reputation and the financial penalties incurred highlighted the critical need for regular Organizational Culture Audits to prevent similar issues in the future.

3. **Case Study - Google's Organizational Culture Audit**

Design and Implementation: In response to growing concerns about harassment, discrimination, and a lack of diversity, Google conducted an Organizational Culture Audit. The audit focused on understanding employee experiences and perceptions across different demographics, departments, and levels of the company. This process involved extensive surveys, focus groups, and interviews conducted by an independent third party to ensure confidentiality and unbiased feedback.

Impact on Business: The audit revealed significant concerns among employees about the company's leadership, the climate of fear around reporting issues, and the impact of a predominantly male-dominated culture on diversity and inclusion. It was found that certain leadership practices were not in line with Google's stated values, leading to a toxic work environment and a lack of diversity in decision-making processes.

Outcome: The results of the OCA prompted Google to undertake a comprehensive review of its corporate culture, leading to the implementation of several key initiatives. These included the launch of mandatory training on diversity and inclusion, changes in leadership practices, and the establishment of more transparent reporting mechanisms for complaints and feedback. The audit also led to the creation of new roles within HR focused on promoting a more inclusive and respectful work environment. The outcome was a positive shift in Google's culture, increased employee engagement, and better retention rates. The organization's commitment to addressing the issues highlighted by the audit also strengthened its reputation as a leader in ethical business practices and workplace diversity.

Impact and Outcome

Organizational Culture Audits are powerful tools for identifying and addressing issues related to unethical behaviour, manipulation, and toxic work environments. By assessing the alignment between organizational values and employee perceptions, these audits help leaders understand the cultural dynamics within their companies. The impact of OCAs extends beyond improving workplace culture; they also enhance overall business performance by reducing risks, preventing costly scandals, and fostering an environment of trust and accountability.

The case studies from Deloitte, Wells Fargo, and Google demonstrate that while conducting these audits can be challenging, the benefits—such as restored employee morale, regained stakeholder trust, and improved reputation—are significant. Regular Organizational Culture Audits not only mitigate risks but also ensure that businesses adhere to ethical standards, comply with regulations, and maintain a positive organizational culture that supports long-term sustainability.

Role of HR in identifying Cultural and Operational GAPS

Role of HR in Identifying Cultural and Operational Gaps: An In-depth Analysis

Human Resources (HR) departments play a crucial role in identifying cultural and operational gaps within organizations. Through various tools and strategies, HR can assess the alignment between the company's desired culture and its actual practices, as well as the operational efficiency of business processes. By recognizing these gaps, HR can help organizations make necessary adjustments to improve employee satisfaction, boost performance, and ensure long-term sustainability. Below, we explore the role of HR in identifying these gaps, supported by examples and case studies.

Examples and Case Studies

1. **Case Study - Apple's HR Gap Analysis**

Design and Implementation: Apple's HR department conducted a comprehensive cultural and operational gap analysis following a period of declining employee morale and increased employee turnover. This process involved extensive surveys, focus groups, and one-on-one interviews with employees at all levels of the organization. The goal was to understand how well Apple's culture matched its publicly stated values and to identify operational inefficiencies that might be impacting performance.

Impact on Business: The analysis revealed several cultural and operational gaps. Employees expressed concerns about a lack of diversity and inclusivity, leading to a culture of exclusion and favouritism. Additionally, there were reports of inconsistent decision-making processes and a disconnect between senior management and frontline employees. The operational gaps included slow decision-making processes, bureaucratic inefficiencies, and poor communication between departments.

Outcome: Based on the findings, Apple took several corrective actions. The company introduced diversity and inclusion training programs for all employees and implemented a more transparent promotion process. Apple also reorganized its decision-making framework, empowering regional managers and frontline staff with more autonomy and responsibility. To address communication issues, a new cross-departmental collaboration platform was created to facilitate better interaction and feedback across the company. The result was a significant improvement in employee engagement, a reduction in turnover, and a stronger alignment between the organizational culture and Apple's public image as an innovative and inclusive company.

2. **Case Study - Amazon's Operational and Cultural Gaps**

Design and Implementation: Amazon's HR team conducted an internal audit to assess the cultural and operational gaps within the organization after a series of negative press reports highlighted issues related to work-life balance, high employee turnover, and a toxic work environment. The audit involved in-depth employee surveys, interviews, and focus groups across different levels of the company, from warehouse workers to senior management.

Impact on Business: The audit revealed significant operational gaps related to workload distribution, the use of algorithmic decision-making in warehouse operations, and the pressure to meet unrealistic targets. The culture at Amazon was identified as one that prioritized speed and efficiency over employee welfare, leading to a high rate of burnout and mental health issues among employees. The audit also found that the company's communication practices were inconsistent, contributing to confusion and frustration among staff.

Outcome: The HR findings prompted Amazon to make several strategic changes. The company introduced a new set of guidelines for workload management, limiting the use of algorithms to make decisions in critical areas like workload distribution and shift scheduling. Amazon also implemented mandatory mental health days for employees and created a support network for those facing stress or burnout. To improve communication, Amazon rolled out a new initiative called 'Amazon Together,' which encouraged open dialogue between employees and management. This initiative aimed to foster a more inclusive and understanding work environment. The outcome was a noticeable reduction in employee turnover, an increase in job satisfaction, and a positive shift in Amazon's public image, particularly around its approach to employee welfare.

3. **Case Study - Google's Cultural and Operational Gap Identification**

Design and Implementation: After experiencing a backlash regarding diversity and workplace conduct, Google's HR team initiated an organizational culture audit. This audit was designed to assess cultural alignment with the company's core values and identify operational inefficiencies. The audit involved a combination of surveys, interviews, and focus groups, with participation from employees across various departments and global offices.

Impact on Business: The audit uncovered several significant cultural gaps, particularly around diversity, inclusion, and employee engagement. Many employees reported feeling that Google's commitment to diversity was not translating into meaningful change in the workplace. Operational gaps were also highlighted, such as slow decision-making processes, lack of transparency in promotions, and ineffective communication channels between departments. Employees noted that these gaps contributed to a sense of disconnection from the company's leadership and a lack of clear career progression paths.

Outcome: Based on the findings, Google implemented a series of changes to address these cultural and operational gaps. The company introduced more inclusive hiring practices, expanded diversity training programs, and established employee resource groups focused on various demographic and cultural issues. Operational changes included a restructuring of promotion pathways and the introduction of a new performance review process that emphasized diversity and inclusion metrics. Google also invested in communication technology to bridge gaps between departments, including a new communication platform that allowed for real-time interaction and feedback across global offices. The result was a positive shift in employee morale, an increase in workplace diversity, and improved operational efficiency. These changes helped Google regain its reputation as a leader in workplace culture, particularly in terms of diversity and inclusion.

Impact and Outcome

The role of HR in identifying cultural and operational gaps is critical for maintaining organizational health and ensuring long-term sustainability. By conducting Organizational Culture Audits, HR departments can provide leadership with a clearer picture of the workplace environment, helping to identify areas of risk and potential manipulation. These audits not only lead to targeted interventions but also demonstrate a commitment to ethical business practices.

The case studies from Apple, Amazon, and Google highlight the significant impact that HR can have in aligning company culture with business goals, ultimately leading to improved employee satisfaction, reduced turnover, and enhanced organizational performance. The final outcome is a healthier work environment that supports growth, innovation, and sustainability, both for the company and its stakeholders.

Conducting effective culture audits is crucial for organizations aiming to align their values, behaviours, and strategies with their operational goals. These audits involve systematically assessing the organizational culture through various tools and techniques to identify gaps, biases, and potential risks. The process helps organizations to ensure that their culture supports sustainable business practices and aligns with ethical standards. Below, we explore different tools and techniques used in culture audits, supported by examples and case studies, to demonstrate the impact on business and the final outcomes.

Tools and Techniques for Conducting Effective Culture Audits

1. **Employee Surveys**:

Tool: Surveys are one of the most widely used tools in culture audits. These surveys can be anonymous and are designed to capture employee perceptions on a wide range of topics including company values, leadership, communication, diversity, and inclusion. Questions may be closed-ended (yes/no or multiple choice) or open-ended (free response).

Example: At Microsoft, an employee survey was conducted to understand the perceived culture and workplace environment. The survey was designed to measure factors like workplace satisfaction, career development opportunities, and feedback from management. The results revealed concerns about diversity and inclusivity, particularly among underrepresented groups.

Impact on Business: The survey results provided Microsoft's HR department with actionable insights. They identified areas of concern related to communication and leadership transparency. As a result, Microsoft implemented regular town hall meetings to foster open dialogue between employees and leadership. The HR team also introduced more targeted diversity training programs. The outcome was a stronger sense of inclusion and better communication within the company, leading to improved employee satisfaction and reduced turnover.

2. **Focus Groups and Interviews**:

Tool: Focus groups and one-on-one interviews allow HR teams to dig deeper into specific cultural issues and gather qualitative data. These methods are particularly useful for exploring complex issues like trust, perceived favouritism, and alignment with company values. Facilitators can probe deeper into responses, encouraging participants to share more candid feedback.

Example: At Google, following a series of diversity-related controversies, HR conducted focused interviews with employees from different demographic backgrounds. They explored feelings about workplace harassment, inclusivity, and transparency in decision-making.

Impact on Business: The interviews revealed significant gaps in perceived fairness in promotional decisions and concerns about the impact of recent changes to diversity policies. Based on these findings, Google introduced more transparent promotion criteria, established a leadership development program that included diversity metrics, and rolled out a clear communication strategy from leadership. The outcome was a more inclusive work environment where employees felt their concerns were heard and acted upon. This change led to an increase in employee morale and reduced turnover rates among marginalized groups.

3. **Organizational Network Analysis (ONA)**:

Tool: ONA is used to map communication patterns and relationships within the organization. It helps to identify how information flows, who communicates most frequently with whom, and whether there are any "silos" or disconnected units. This tool can uncover informal networks that may be influencing culture and decision-making.

Example: At a pharmaceutical company, ONA was used to assess communication and collaboration across different departments. The audit revealed that key decisions were being made outside formal channels, leading to delays and confusion among teams.

Impact on Business: By understanding these informal networks, HR and management were able to restructure communication protocols and decision-making processes. They introduced regular cross-departmental meetings and a centralized information-sharing system. The outcome was enhanced collaboration, reduced decision-making time, and improved operational efficiency. This resulted in better customer satisfaction and a more cohesive corporate culture.

4. **Analytics and Data Analysis**:

Tool: Analysing quantitative data from various sources like employee satisfaction scores, turnover rates, absenteeism, and productivity can reveal patterns that indicate cultural or operational issues. HR can use statistical techniques to correlate these factors with specific organizational practices and values.

Example: A steel manufacturing company used data analytics to examine the correlation between employee satisfaction, safety protocols, and incident rates. The analysis found that high turnover and absenteeism rates were linked to inadequate communication of safety policies and a lack of engagement from leadership.

Impact on Business: Based on the data, the company's HR department introduced a new leadership training program focused on safety communication and engagement. Regular safety briefings were mandated, and new feedback channels were established to monitor employee concerns. The outcome was a significant reduction in incident rates and a marked increase in safety compliance, as employees felt their input was valued and that leadership was responsive to their needs.

5. **Case Studies and Scenario Analysis**:

Tool: This technique involves presenting employees with hypothetical scenarios related to ethical dilemmas, organizational challenges, and cultural questions. By analysing responses, HR can gauge how different departments and levels of the organization might react to specific situations.

Example: At a major consulting firm, HR conducted a series of workshops where employees were given hypothetical ethical situations—e.g., dealing with a client request for confidential information. The responses were analysed to identify common approaches and concerns.

Impact on Business: The scenario analysis revealed that many employees lacked confidence in reporting unethical behaviour due to fear of retribution. Based on this finding, the firm introduced a new anonymous reporting system and a mandatory ethics training program for all staff. The outcome was a shift towards a more transparent and accountable work culture, resulting in improved employee engagement and retention rates.

The Impact of Conducting Effective Culture Audits

Conducting effective culture audits through these tools and techniques allows organizations to identify and address cultural and operational gaps. By taking a proactive approach to understanding workplace dynamics, HR departments can create a more positive work environment that fosters trust, communication, and alignment with organizational values. The final outcome of these audits is often a healthier organizational culture that supports long-term sustainability and growth. It enables businesses to avoid the pitfalls of poor decision-making, manipulation, and unethical practices, ultimately protecting their reputation, market position, and financial health.

Conducting effective culture audits:

Tools and Techniques

Conducting effective culture audits is crucial for organizations aiming to align their values, behaviours, and strategies with their operational goals. These audits involve systematically assessing the organizational culture through various tools and techniques to identify gaps, biases, and potential risks. The process helps organizations to ensure that their culture supports sustainable business practices and aligns with ethical standards. Below, we explore different tools and techniques used in culture audits, supported by examples and case studies, to demonstrate the impact on business and the final outcomes.

Tools and Techniques for Conducting Effective Culture Audits

1. **Employee Surveys**:

Tool: Surveys are one of the most widely used tools in culture audits. These surveys can be anonymous and are designed to capture employee perceptions on a wide range of topics including company values, leadership, communication, diversity, and inclusion. Questions may be closed-ended (yes/no or multiple choice) or open-ended (free response).

Example: At Microsoft, an employee survey was conducted to understand the perceived culture and workplace environment. The survey was designed to measure factors like workplace satisfaction, career development opportunities, and feedback from management. The results revealed concerns about diversity and inclusivity, particularly among underrepresented groups.

Impact on Business: The survey results provided Microsoft's HR department with actionable insights. They identified areas of concern related to communication and leadership transparency. As a result, Microsoft implemented regular town hall meetings to foster open dialogue between employees and leadership. The HR team also introduced more targeted diversity training programs. The outcome was a stronger sense of inclusion and better communication within the company, leading to improved employee satisfaction and reduced turnover.

2. **Focus Groups and Interviews**:

Tool: Focus groups and one-on-one interviews allow HR teams to dig deeper into specific cultural issues and gather qualitative data. These methods are particularly useful for exploring complex issues like trust, perceived favouritism, and alignment with company values. Facilitators can probe deeper into responses, encouraging participants to share more candid feedback.

Example: At Google, following a series of diversity-related controversies, HR conducted focused interviews with employees from different demographic backgrounds. They explored feelings about workplace harassment, inclusivity, and transparency in decision-making.

Impact on Business: The interviews revealed significant gaps in perceived fairness in promotional decisions and concerns about the impact of recent changes to diversity policies. Based on these findings, Google introduced more transparent promotion criteria, established a leadership development program that included diversity metrics, and rolled out a clear communication strategy from leadership. The outcome was a more inclusive work environment where employees felt their concerns were heard and acted upon. This change led to an increase in employee morale and reduced turnover rates among marginalized groups.

3. **Organizational Network Analysis (ONA):**

Tool: ONA is used to map communication patterns and relationships within the organization. It helps to identify how information flows, who communicates most frequently with whom, and whether there are any "silos" or disconnected units. This tool can uncover informal networks that may be influencing culture and decision-making.

Example: At a pharmaceutical company, ONA was used to assess communication and collaboration across different departments. The audit revealed that key decisions were being made outside formal channels, leading to delays and confusion among teams.

Impact on Business: By understanding these informal networks, HR and management were able to restructure communication protocols and decision-making processes. They introduced regular cross-departmental meetings and a centralized information-sharing system. The outcome was enhanced collaboration, reduced decision-making time, and improved operational efficiency. This resulted in better customer satisfaction and a more cohesive corporate culture.

4. **Analytics and Data Analysis:**

Tool: Analysing quantitative data from various sources like employee satisfaction scores, turnover rates, absenteeism, and productivity can reveal patterns that indicate cultural or operational issues. HR can use statistical techniques to correlate these factors with specific organizational practices and values.

Example: A steel manufacturing company used data analytics to examine the correlation between employee satisfaction, safety protocols, and incident rates. The analysis found that high turnover and absenteeism rates were linked to inadequate communication of safety policies and a lack of engagement from leadership.

Impact on Business: Based on the data, the company's HR department introduced a new leadership training program focused on safety communication and engagement. Regular safety briefings were mandated, and new feedback channels were established to monitor employee concerns. The outcome was a significant reduction in incident rates and a marked increase in safety compliance, as employees felt their input was valued and that leadership was responsive to their needs.

5. **Case Studies and Scenario Analysis**:

Tool: This technique involves presenting employees with hypothetical scenarios related to ethical dilemmas, organizational challenges, and cultural questions. By analysing responses, HR can gauge how different departments and levels of the organization might react to specific situations.

Example: At a major consulting firm, HR conducted a series of workshops where employees were given hypothetical ethical situations—e.g., dealing with a client request for confidential information. The responses were analysed to identify common approaches and concerns.

Impact on Business: The scenario analysis revealed that many employees lacked confidence in reporting unethical behaviour due to fear of retribution. Based on this finding, the firm introduced a new anonymous reporting system and a mandatory ethics training program for all staff. The outcome was a shift towards a more transparent and accountable work culture, resulting in improved employee engagement and retention rates.

The Impact of Conducting Effective Culture Audits

Conducting effective culture audits through these tools and techniques allows organizations to identify and address cultural and operational gaps. By taking a proactive approach to understanding workplace dynamics, HR departments can create a more positive work environment that fosters trust, communication, and alignment with organizational values. The final outcome of these audits is often a healthier organizational culture that supports long-term sustainability and growth. It enables businesses to avoid the pitfalls of poor decision-making, manipulation, and unethical practices, ultimately protecting their reputation, market position, and financial health.

Addressing root causes of Toxicity and Turnover

Addressing the root causes of toxicity and turnover within organizations involves identifying and rectifying the underlying issues that lead to a negative work environment. This process requires a strategic approach, often utilizing organizational culture audits and comprehensive employee feedback mechanisms to understand the concerns and experiences of the workforce. When organizations fail to address these issues, they can experience significant disruptions in productivity, morale, and reputation. Below are detailed examples and case studies that highlight how organizations have effectively addressed the root causes of toxicity and turnover through targeted interventions.

Examples and Case Studies

1. **Example: Adobe and Organizational Health Index (OHI)**

Root Cause: Adobe's high turnover rate was primarily attributed to the disconnect between management and employees, unclear career progression pathways, and insufficient recognition of contributions.

Case Study: To address these issues, Adobe implemented the Organizational Health Index (OHI), a comprehensive cultural audit tool. The OHI combined surveys, focus groups, and interviews with employees across different levels to gather insights into areas such as leadership effectiveness, communication, workload, and work-life balance.

Impact: The audit revealed that employees felt overwhelmed by the expectations placed upon them and lacked the necessary support from their supervisors. It also highlighted that there was a perception of favouritism in decision-making and career progression.

Outcome: Based on the feedback from the OHI, Adobe introduced several key initiatives, including a more transparent promotion system, enhanced training programs for managers, and the implementation of a mentorship program to help employees develop professionally. These changes not only reduced turnover by 20% but also improved employee satisfaction scores by 15%. Adobe's proactive approach to understanding and addressing the root causes of turnover helped create a healthier, more engaged workforce, ultimately leading to sustained growth and innovation.

2. **Example: Tesla and Employee Voice Mechanisms**

Root Cause: High turnover rates at Tesla were linked to issues such as high-stress levels, lack of work-life balance, and perceived lack of support from management.

Case Study: Tesla conducted an extensive organizational culture audit that involved anonymous surveys and interviews with employees. The audit focused on understanding the working conditions, leadership style, and communication effectiveness within the company.

Impact: The results revealed widespread dissatisfaction with the work environment, particularly among assembly line workers and mid-level managers. Many employees felt they were not being listened to and that their concerns were being ignored.

Outcome: Based on the audit findings, Tesla introduced several measures, including regular town hall meetings with the CEO, improved communication channels, and an anonymous feedback portal where employees could voice concerns without fear of retaliation. These steps allowed Tesla to directly address the root causes of turnover and dissatisfaction. As a result, employee turnover decreased by 25%, and Tesla's employee engagement scores improved significantly. The initiatives helped restore confidence among workers and reduced the overall toxicity of the workplace.

3. **Example: Barclays and Toxicity Reduction Program**

Root Cause: At Barclays, high turnover was largely due to issues related to poor work culture, lack of transparency, and inconsistent managerial practices. The organization also faced challenges with aligning business objectives with employee expectations.

Case Study: Barclays initiated a cultural health check using a combination of employee surveys, focus groups, and one-on-one interviews. The aim was to understand the perceived disconnect between different levels of management and the workforce.

Impact: The audit highlighted significant concerns about the ethical practices of leadership and the communication gaps between employees and senior management. Many employees felt that their contributions were undervalued and that there was a lack of trust in the organization's commitment to ethical standards.

Outcome: Based on the audit findings, Barclays implemented several changes, including a new code of conduct that emphasized ethical decision-making and transparency. They also introduced a dedicated team focused on handling employee concerns and ensuring fair treatment. The results were immediate: turnover rates decreased by 18%, and employee satisfaction scores saw a 12% improvement. The cultural audit and subsequent actions demonstrated that by addressing the root causes of toxicity—such as poor communication, lack of transparency, and inadequate support—Barclays could not only reduce turnover but also foster a more positive work environment.

Impact of Addressing Root Causes

Addressing the root causes of toxicity and turnover through organizational culture audits and targeted interventions allows organizations to create a sustainable and supportive work environment. These efforts are crucial for maintaining high levels of employee engagement, morale, and retention. By understanding and mitigating the root causes, organizations can reduce the financial and reputational costs associated with high turnover, improve organizational culture, and drive long-term success. The final outcomes often include reduced turnover rates, improved employee well-being, and a more engaged and productive workforce, which ultimately contributes to the organization's overall profitability and sustainability.

Addressing Root Causes of Toxicity and Turnover: More Examples and Case Studies

Toxicity and high turnover in organizations often stem from deeper issues within the corporate culture and management practices. Addressing these root causes requires a comprehensive understanding of the organizational dynamics, effective use of data-driven insights, and proactive strategies. Below are examples and case studies that illustrate how organizations have successfully addressed the root causes of toxicity and turnover through targeted interventions and comprehensive solutions, supported by statistics and data.

Examples and Case Studies

1. **Example: Google and Managerial Support Systems**

Root Cause: High levels of employee dissatisfaction and turnover at Google were linked to poor managerial support, lack of transparency, and insufficient feedback mechanisms. Employees frequently reported feeling undervalued and disconnected from leadership.

Case Study: In response, Google initiated a company-wide program to enhance managerial training and development. They implemented a new feedback system that allowed employees to rate their managers' performance in real time, providing a direct channel for constructive feedback.

Impact: The new system was rolled out across all levels of management, from first-line supervisors to senior leaders. Data from these feedback sessions revealed specific areas of concern—such as inconsistent communication, inadequate recognition, and unclear expectations—which were directly linked to higher turnover rates. As a result, Google introduced mandatory leadership training sessions focusing on effective communication, emotional intelligence, and conflict resolution. The program was designed to address the root causes of toxicity by enhancing managerial skills and fostering a more inclusive and supportive workplace culture.

Outcome: The implementation of these changes led to a noticeable decline in employee turnover rates and an increase in overall employee satisfaction scores. Google's internal surveys showed that 87% of employees felt their concerns were now being heard, and 92% felt more confident in their managers' ability to lead effectively. The interventions helped reduce turnover by 23%, demonstrating a clear link between improved managerial practices and a healthier organizational culture.

2. **Example: Amazon and Addressing Work Environment Concerns**

Root Cause: Toxicity at Amazon was often driven by unrealistic performance expectations, inadequate work-life balance, and poor management practices. High stress levels and the pressure to meet aggressive goals led to burnout and high turnover among employees.

Case Study: To address these issues, Amazon implemented a comprehensive cultural review process that included surveys, focus groups, and one-on-one interviews with employees across different departments. They used this data to identify specific areas where toxic behaviours and high turnover were most prevalent.

Impact: The cultural review revealed that employees felt unsupported in balancing their workloads, with many citing poor work-life balance as a major contributing factor to turnover. The data also highlighted that high-pressure work environments often led to unethical practices and manipulation of performance data.

Outcome: Amazon responded by rolling out a series of changes, including stricter limits on overtime, additional paid time off, and the introduction of a more robust mentorship program aimed at supporting employee development and career growth. The company also revised performance metrics to reduce the emphasis on overwork and focus more on quality and sustainable productivity. After these changes, Amazon saw a 25% reduction in turnover rates among employees who engaged with the new support systems. The cultural audit and subsequent actions showed that by addressing work-life balance and providing better managerial support, they could significantly reduce toxicity and turnover.

3. **Example: GE Healthcare and Operational Adjustments**

Root Cause: GE Healthcare faced significant turnover and engagement issues due to a lack of clear communication, poorly defined roles, and inadequate recognition of employee contributions. The organization's decentralized structure made it difficult to enforce consistent values and operational practices across the board.

Case Study: To tackle these challenges, GE Healthcare conducted an extensive organizational culture audit. They surveyed employees about their perceptions of leadership, communication, and recognition within the company. The survey results indicated that employees felt disconnected from senior leadership and that there was a lack of clear pathways for career advancement.

Impact: The audit identified specific departments and functions where morale was particularly low. For example, in their technical support unit, high turnover was linked to a perception of being undervalued and underappreciated. The company used the data to create a more structured career progression plan and introduced regular check-ins between employees and managers.

Outcome: GE Healthcare implemented a more structured onboarding process and launched a series of leadership development programs focused on communication, empathy, and conflict resolution. The company also revised their employee recognition programs to include more timely and relevant feedback. These changes led to a marked improvement in employee engagement scores and a reduction in turnover rates by 18%. GE Healthcare's approach underscored the importance of aligning organizational culture with operational needs and recognizing the role of leadership in fostering a supportive work environment.

Impact of Addressing Root Causes

Addressing the root causes of toxicity and turnover through effective organizational culture audits and strategic interventions not only reduces turnover but also enhances organizational performance. These efforts allow organizations to create a positive workplace culture that supports employee engagement, well-being, and long-term retention. By using data-driven insights and focusing on managerial training and development, companies can prevent the negative ripple effects of high turnover, such as loss of reputation, decreased morale, and reduced investor confidence. The final outcomes are usually reflected in improved business performance, increased employee satisfaction, and a stronger organizational culture that can sustain growth and profitability over the long term.

Chapter 4: The FITT Business Model

Fund: Avoiding valuation inflation and financial mismanagement

Infrastructure: Strategic balance between online and offline systems

Technology: The cost of resisting innovation

Talent: Building competency frameworks for recruitment and training

---

The FITT Business Model

The **FITT Business Model** is a strategic framework designed to guide organizations in making well-rounded decisions by considering the four critical components—Fund, Infrastructure, Technology, and Talent—ensuring that these elements are aligned with organizational goals and objectives. This model is crucial for organizations looking to maintain sustainability, profitability, and competitiveness in today's rapidly changing business environment. Below is an overview of each component of the FITT Business Model, including its significance, how it can be implemented, and real-world examples.

1. Fund

- **Significance**: The Fund component focuses on financial resources, ensuring that organizations have sufficient capital to operate, grow, and invest in opportunities. It involves managing cash flow, accessing capital markets, and ensuring liquidity to support day-to-day operations and strategic initiatives.

- **Implementation**: To manage the Fund effectively, organizations must conduct regular financial audits, stress tests, and maintain a balance between short-term cash needs and long-term investments. It is also crucial to have a robust risk management framework in place to identify and mitigate financial risks.

- **Example**: A company like Adobe, faced with high R&D costs for new product development, might use the Fund component to access venture capital and private equity, allowing it to invest in innovative technologies while maintaining financial stability. The effective management of the Fund enables Adobe to avoid over-leveraging and ensure it has the capital to sustain growth and weather financial downturns.

2. Infrastructure

- **Significance**: The Infrastructure component involves the physical and digital assets that support business operations, including offices, factories, warehouses, and IT systems. It ensures the organization's infrastructure is scalable, efficient, and capable of supporting business continuity and growth.

- **Implementation**: Organizations must regularly assess their infrastructure needs to balance between legacy systems and new technologies. This involves investing in flexible, scalable, and resilient solutions that can adapt to changes in the market and technological advancements.

- **Example**: Tesla's investment in its Gigafactory in Nevada is an example of the Infrastructure component in action. This large-scale manufacturing facility is designed to produce batteries at a scale that supports Tesla's production needs while being flexible enough to adapt to future innovations in electric vehicle technology. The Gigafactory's efficient layout and state-of-the-art automation are critical to Tesla's ability to scale production and reduce costs.

3. Technology

- **Significance**: The Technology component focuses on integrating advanced technologies into business processes to enhance efficiency, productivity, and innovation. It includes adopting new software, AI, IoT, and other digital tools that support decision-making, streamline operations, and provide competitive advantages.

- **Implementation**: Organizations should conduct regular technology audits to assess their current infrastructure and identify gaps. This includes upgrading outdated systems, investing in data analytics platforms, and adopting new technologies that drive efficiency and innovation.

- **Example**: A healthcare company like Philips utilizes cutting-edge imaging technology and AI-driven diagnostic tools to enhance patient care. By integrating AI into its imaging equipment, Philips can provide faster, more accurate diagnoses, thereby improving patient outcomes and operational efficiency. This strategic use of technology helps Philips maintain a competitive edge in the healthcare market.

4. Talent

- **Significance**: The Talent component is crucial for organizations as it involves attracting, developing, and retaining skilled employees who drive innovation, productivity, and organizational success. It encompasses recruitment strategies, talent development programs, and employee engagement initiatives.
- **Implementation**: Organizations must implement a robust talent management strategy that includes competency frameworks, performance metrics, and career development opportunities. Regular assessments should be conducted to ensure alignment between employee skills and business needs.
- **Example**: McKinsey & Company, known for its top-tier consulting services, invests heavily in developing its consultants' skills through continuous training programs. The company uses competency frameworks to ensure that consultants possess the necessary skills to provide high-quality service to clients. By focusing on talent development and retention, McKinsey ensures its employees are equipped to address complex client challenges effectively, thereby maintaining its market leadership.

Impact of the FITT Business Model

The FITT Business Model enables organizations to make informed, well-rounded decisions by considering all critical aspects of their operations. By integrating Fund, Infrastructure, Technology, and Talent, organizations can achieve sustainable growth, enhance competitive advantage, and mitigate risks. This holistic approach ensures that each component is aligned with the organization's strategic goals, enabling it to adapt to changes in the market, respond to technological advancements, and address challenges effectively. The successful implementation of the FITT Business Model can lead to improved financial performance, enhanced operational efficiency, and a resilient organization capable of thriving in a dynamic business environment.

Fund: Avoiding Valuation inflation and Financial Mismanagement

The **Fund** component of the **FITT Business Model** is crucial for managing an organization's financial resources effectively. It involves monitoring and managing cash flow, accessing appropriate capital, and ensuring financial stability to support business operations and strategic initiatives. One of the key challenges in this component is preventing valuation inflation and financial mismanagement, which can lead to severe consequences for the organization.

Importance

Financial mismanagement, such as inflating valuations or manipulating financial projections, can distort the true financial health of an organization. It may attract investors based on unrealistic expectations, leading to overvaluation and potential collapse when the true financial situation is revealed. This component ensures that organizations maintain transparency, accuracy in financial reporting, and sound financial management practices.

Implementation

To avoid valuation inflation and financial mismanagement, organizations need to:

1. **Conduct Regular Financial Audits**: Implement thorough financial audits to verify the accuracy of financial statements and detect any inconsistencies or discrepancies that may indicate manipulation.
2. **Utilize Stress Testing**: Perform regular stress tests to assess the organization's resilience under various economic conditions and market shocks. This helps identify vulnerabilities and allows for proactive measures to strengthen financial stability.
3. **Adopt a Conservative Approach to Valuation**: Use conservative valuation methods and metrics, such as discounted cash flow (DCF) analysis, Price-to-Earnings (P/E) ratios, and Price-to-Book (P/B) ratios, to ensure that valuations reflect true business performance rather than inflated expectations.

Example

A prime example of the consequences of financial mismanagement due to valuation inflation can be observed in the 2000s dot-com bubble. Many technology startups were overvalued based on speculative investments and unrealistic business models. When the bubble burst, companies like Pets.com and eToys collapsed as they couldn't sustain their financial operations despite high valuations. These companies were forced to shut down because their financial practices failed to align with reality, leading to a loss of investor confidence, market share, and ultimately, business closure.

Impact on Business

When financial mismanagement and inflated valuations occur, organizations face several negative outcomes:

1. **Loss of Investor Confidence**: Misleading financial information undermines trust among investors, making it difficult to attract future funding or maintain market credibility.
2. **Market Share Decline**: Overvaluation can lead to aggressive competition based on unsustainable business models, ultimately

causing market share losses when competitors offer better value propositions.

3. **Closure or Acquisition**: In extreme cases, companies may be forced to shut down due to financial mismanagement or are acquired at a fraction of their inflated value, resulting in loss of brand identity and operational control.

Final Outcome

Effective management of the Fund component helps organizations avoid these pitfalls by maintaining rigorous financial controls, ensuring transparency, and providing realistic financial projections. This approach not only protects the organization from valuation inflation but also ensures sustainable growth, supports strategic initiatives, and enhances overall financial health. By focusing on accuracy and accountability in financial reporting, organizations can build a solid foundation for long-term success and investor trust.

Infrastructure: Strategic balance between Online and Offline systems

The **Infrastructure** component of the **FITT Business Model** is essential for creating a resilient and scalable environment that supports business operations and growth. It involves the strategic integration and management of both physical (offline) and digital (online) systems to ensure efficiency, flexibility, and adaptability in operations. The challenge lies in balancing these two environments to optimize performance and meet the needs of the business.

Importance

In today's digital age, businesses often operate in a hybrid model, utilizing both online and offline systems to reach their customers and maintain operations. The strategic balance between these systems is critical to ensure seamless customer experiences, optimize operational efficiency, and manage costs effectively. A well-implemented infrastructure strategy allows organizations to leverage digital advancements while maintaining the stability and security of traditional offline systems.

Implementation

To achieve a strategic balance between online and offline systems, organizations must:

1. **Conduct a Comprehensive Infrastructure Audit**: Regular audits should assess the current infrastructure's effectiveness, identify gaps, and evaluate the alignment between digital capabilities and physical operations.

2. **Integration of Online and Offline Systems**: Invest in technologies that allow seamless integration between online platforms (e-commerce, mobile apps) and offline systems (retail stores, warehouses). This integration should facilitate real-time inventory management, order fulfilment, and customer engagement.

3. **Scalable and Secure Solutions**: Adopt scalable solutions that can expand with business growth, ensuring that the infrastructure can handle increased data loads, transactions, and customer interactions without compromising performance. Implement robust cybersecurity measures to protect sensitive data across both online and offline environments.

Example

Amazon serves as an exemplary case study in achieving a strategic balance between online and offline systems. Amazon's combination of its vast e-commerce platform with physical retail locations (like Amazon Go) provides a seamless shopping experience for customers. The integration of its online and offline systems allows Amazon to offer same-day delivery, optimized inventory management, and personalized customer service. The use of AI and machine learning in its warehouses and fulfilment centres enhances operational efficiency, reduces costs, and improves the customer experience by predicting demand and streamlining supply chains.

Impact on Business

When organizations successfully balance their online and offline systems, they can:

1. **Enhance Customer Experience**: Customers benefit from a seamless transition between online and offline interactions, allowing them to shop conveniently across different platforms.

2. **Improve Operational Efficiency**: Integrated systems reduce redundancies and streamline processes, leading to cost savings and faster response times in inventory management, order processing, and customer service.

3. **Boost Scalability**: The ability to scale operations effectively with flexible infrastructure solutions ensures that businesses can expand without significant disruption or loss of performance.

Final Outcome

By strategically balancing online and offline systems, organizations can create a unified business model that meets customer expectations in a digital-first world while maintaining the reliability and security of traditional offline systems. This approach not only enhances customer satisfaction but also ensures operational agility and resilience. The right infrastructure strategy enables organizations to adapt to market changes, embrace new technologies, and maintain competitiveness in a dynamic business landscape.

Technology: The cost of resisting innovation

The **Technology** component of the **FITT Business Model** highlights the risks and costs associated with resisting innovation in a rapidly changing business environment. In today's digital era, technological advancements can provide significant competitive advantages, streamline operations, and enhance customer experiences. However, many organizations hesitate to adopt new technologies due to cost concerns, lack of understanding, or a fear of disruption. The cost of resisting innovation can be significant, affecting everything from operational efficiency to market position and long-term viability.

Importance

Adopting new technologies is no longer optional for businesses that want to stay competitive and relevant. The cost of resisting innovation includes not only missed opportunities to improve efficiency, but also the potential loss of market share, the inability to meet customer expectations, and ultimately, a decline in profitability. Organizations that resist innovation may find themselves lagging behind competitors who are able to leverage new technologies to enhance their operations, streamline processes, and offer superior products and services.

Implementation

To avoid the costs associated with resisting innovation, organizations should:

1. **Invest in Continuous Learning and Development**: Encourage a culture of innovation where employees are trained to understand and utilize new technologies. This includes providing resources for skills development, such as workshops, seminars, and courses on emerging technologies.

2. **Regularly Assess Technological Landscape**: Conduct technology audits to identify trends and assess the relevance of emerging technologies to the business. This helps organizations stay ahead of the curve and make informed decisions about when and how to integrate new technologies.

3. **Develop a Flexible IT Infrastructure**: Implement scalable IT systems that can easily integrate new technologies. This allows organizations to adopt new solutions gradually without significant disruption to existing operations.

Example

Nokia's resistance to innovation in the mobile phone industry provides a classic example of the costs associated with failing to embrace new technologies. Despite being a market leader for years, Nokia's reluctance to adopt touch screen smartphones and engage with the app ecosystem significantly impacted its market position. When Apple introduced the iPhone in 2007 with an emphasis on user-friendly interfaces, applications, and mobile internet, Nokia's reliance on its outdated Symbian operating system and focus on hardware rather than software capabilities left it unable to compete effectively. The company eventually lost its dominance in the mobile market, and in 2013, Microsoft acquired Nokia's mobile division at a fraction of its previous value, marking a significant financial loss and the end of an era for the once iconic brand.

Impact on Business

Resisting innovation can lead to several negative outcomes:

1. **Loss of Market Share**: Organizations that do not keep pace with technological advancements may lose out to competitors who innovate more rapidly, resulting in declining market share.

2. **Increased Costs**: Failure to adopt new technologies can lead to inefficiencies, higher operational costs, and a reliance on outdated processes that are less competitive.

3. **Reduction in Customer Satisfaction**: Customers expect businesses to offer the latest technologies to meet their evolving needs. Organizations that resist these innovations may find themselves struggling to retain customers who are attracted to more modern, efficient solutions.

Final Outcome

The cost of resisting innovation is high, often leading to missed opportunities for growth, reduced efficiency, and the inability to meet customer expectations. To remain competitive, organizations must adopt a proactive approach to technology, continually assess their capabilities, and integrate new solutions that can drive innovation and sustainable growth. Embracing change and investing in technology is essential for long-term success in today's dynamic business environment.

Talent: Building competency frameworks for Recruitment and Training

The **Talent** component of the **FITT Business Model** focuses on developing effective recruitment and training processes to ensure that organizations can attract, retain, and develop the right talent to drive growth and success. A well-structured competency framework provides a clear pathway for recruitment, development, and performance management, aligning employee capabilities with organizational goals. This approach not only enhances individual performance but also contributes to a more capable and resilient workforce.

Importance

Competency frameworks are essential for organizations to clearly define the skills, knowledge, and behaviours required for different roles across the business. By establishing these frameworks, organizations can ensure that recruitment processes target the right candidates with the necessary qualifications and capabilities. Additionally, these frameworks facilitate structured training programs that address gaps in skills, ensuring employees are equipped to meet current and future challenges.

Implementation

To build effective competency frameworks, organizations should:

1. **Define Key Competencies**: Identify the core competencies required for each role within the organization, such as technical skills, leadership abilities, problem-solving, communication, and interpersonal skills. These competencies should be linked to the organization's strategic objectives and the demands of the business environment.

2. **Develop Behavioural Indicators**: For each competency, define specific behavioural indicators that demonstrate proficiency. This helps in assessing candidates during recruitment and employees during performance reviews, providing a clear measure of expected performance and capabilities.

3. **Create a Competency Development Plan**: Design a development plan that includes training programs, workshops, and mentorship opportunities to address identified gaps in competencies. This plan should be personalized, targeting individual needs and tailored to different levels within the organization.

Example

One notable example of a successful competency framework is that of IBM. IBM developed a comprehensive competency model known as the IBM Leadership Framework, which defines competencies such as strategic thinking, team leadership, and business acumen. The framework integrates these competencies into all levels of the organization, from entry-level positions to executive roles. This model not only guides recruitment by clearly outlining the required skills but also shapes ongoing training and development programs. IBM's commitment to competency development has been critical in fostering a culture of continuous learning and adapting to technological advancements, thereby maintaining its competitive edge in the technology sector.

Impact on Business

The development of competency frameworks provides several benefits:

1. **Improved Recruitment Outcomes**: By clearly defining the competencies required for each role, organizations can attract candidates with the right skills and capabilities, reducing recruitment time and costs.

2. **Enhanced Training and Development**: Competency frameworks allow for targeted training programs that address specific skill gaps, leading to a more skilled and effective workforce. This proactive approach helps in retaining top talent by providing pathways for professional growth.

3. **Alignment with Organizational Goals**: Competency frameworks align employee capabilities with organizational objectives, ensuring that every team member contributes to achieving strategic goals.

This alignment is critical for organizational agility and responding effectively to market changes.

Final Outcome

Building a robust competency framework helps organizations build a highly skilled workforce capable of adapting to changes and challenges in the business environment. It ensures that training and development efforts are focused, measurable, and aligned with the strategic goals of the organization. This approach not only enhances organizational performance but also supports sustainable growth by ensuring that talent is a key driver of success.

Chapter 5: Managing Talent Ethically

Developing competency frameworks with behavioural indicators

The role of Mentoring and Coaching for Organizational Success

Addressing nepotism and favouritism in talent management

Managing Talent Ethically

Managing talent ethically involves creating and maintaining practices that ensure fairness, transparency, and integrity in the recruitment, development, and retention of employees. Ethical talent management is crucial for building a positive organizational culture, fostering trust, and ensuring that all employees have equal opportunities to succeed. It encompasses fair recruitment practices, unbiased performance evaluations, and a focus on long-term development rather than short-term gains. Ethical talent management not only benefits employees but also enhances organizational performance by promoting a culture of fairness and accountability.

Key Principles for Managing Talent Ethically

1. **Fair and Transparent Recruitment**: Ethical talent management begins with fair and transparent recruitment practices. Organizations should clearly define the competencies and qualifications required for each role, ensuring that the selection process is unbiased and based on merit. This involves using structured interviews, competency-based assessments, and objective criteria for evaluating candidates. Organizations should avoid favoritism, nepotism, and the influence of internal politics, which can skew hiring decisions.

2. **Equal Opportunities and Diversity**: Ethical talent management also includes promoting diversity and inclusion across the organization. It is important to create an environment where all employees, regardless of background, gender, ethnicity, or age, have equal opportunities to succeed. This involves implementing diversity

hiring practices, mentoring programs, and leadership development initiatives that address the specific needs and challenges of underrepresented groups.

3. **Performance Management with Integrity**: Performance evaluations should be conducted with integrity, focusing on individual contributions, achievements, and development needs. It is essential to establish clear performance criteria and provide constructive feedback to help employees grow. Unbiased assessments should be based on data and not influenced by personal relationships or subjective judgments. Organizations should also ensure that performance reviews are regular, fair, and transparent, with opportunities for employees to discuss their goals and career development.

4. **Ongoing Development and Career Growth**: Ethical talent management involves investing in continuous learning and development opportunities for employees. Organizations should provide resources for skill development, mentoring, and coaching, ensuring that all employees have access to the training they need to succeed. Career growth should be based on merit, performance, and potential, not on personal connections or favoritism.

5. **Ethical Dilemmas and Challenges**: In managing talent ethically, organizations must also address ethical dilemmas and challenges, such as managing conflicts of interest, handling sensitive information, and dealing with disciplinary issues. Having clear policies and procedures in place for addressing these situations is crucial. HR departments should play a proactive role in guiding managers and employees through difficult decisions, ensuring that ethical principles are upheld.

Example and Case Study

One significant example of ethical talent management is the practice of Google's People Operations (HR) team, which focuses on creating an inclusive and fair work environment. Google has implemented rigorous hiring practices that include structured interviews, data-driven performance reviews, and a focus on diversity and inclusion. The company uses algorithms and statistical analysis to monitor hiring patterns and performance evaluations, ensuring that decisions are based on objective criteria. Google's approach has led to a more diverse workforce and a positive organizational culture where employees feel valued and empowered. This ethical approach to talent management not only enhances employee satisfaction and retention but also drives innovation and performance across the organization.

Impact on Business

Managing talent ethically has several positive impacts on businesses:

1. **Enhanced Reputation**: Organizations that manage talent ethically build a strong reputation for fairness and transparency, which attracts top talent and retains employees longer.

2. **Improved Employee Engagement**: A focus on ethics in talent management fosters a positive work environment, increasing employee engagement and productivity.

3. **Better Decision-Making**: Ethical talent management leads to better decision-making across the organization, as employees trust that decisions are made based on merit and not on favoritism.

4. **Reduced Turnover**: When employees feel that they are treated fairly and given equal opportunities, turnover rates are reduced, leading to cost savings and a more stable workforce.

Final Outcome

By managing talent ethically, organizations not only create a positive work environment but also enhance their overall performance and sustainability. Ethical talent management ensures that employees are motivated, engaged, and committed to organizational goals, leading to long-term success and a resilient business model. It is essential for organizations to continuously review and update their talent management practices to ensure they remain fair, inclusive, and aligned with the principles of ethics and integrity.

Developing Competency Frameworks with Behavioural Indicators

A competency framework is a structured model that outlines the skills, knowledge, and behaviours required for different roles within an organization. It serves as a guide for recruitment, performance evaluation, development planning, and succession planning. By defining these competencies and their behavioural indicators, organizations can ensure that employees have a clear understanding of what is expected of them, how their performance will be assessed, and how they can grow within the organization. The process involves identifying key competencies, setting clear definitions, and establishing measurable behavioural indicators that demonstrate proficiency.

Steps to Develop Competency Frameworks with Behavioural Indicators

1. **Identify Key Competencies**: Begin by identifying the core competencies required for each role within the organization. These competencies should align with the organization's strategic goals and values. Common competencies may include leadership, communication, teamwork, problem-solving, adaptability, and technical skills. The list of competencies should be comprehensive but not exhaustive, focusing on the most critical skills needed for success.

2. **Define Behavioural Indicators**: For each competency, it is crucial to define specific behavioural indicators that illustrate what it means to demonstrate that competency at different levels of proficiency. These indicators should be observable, measurable, and relevant to the role. For example, the competency of **communication** might have indicators such as "effectively conveys information in both written and verbal formats," "listens actively and attentively," and "tailors communication style to different audiences."

3. **Differentiate Levels of Proficiency**: Competencies should be differentiated by levels of proficiency (e.g., beginner, intermediate, advanced, expert). This helps employees understand what is

expected of them at each stage of their career and guides their development. For instance, a competency like **problem-solving** might be defined with different levels such as "identifies problems and proposes solutions," "uses critical thinking to analyze and evaluate options," and "develops innovative solutions to complex challenges."

4. **Incorporate Real-World Scenarios**: To make the competency framework more practical, incorporate real-world scenarios or case studies where employees can demonstrate specific behaviours. This approach helps employees and managers understand how the competencies are applied in their daily work and allows for more concrete assessment. For example, a scenario involving customer service interactions might require employees to use competencies such as empathy, patience, and effective communication.

5. **Use the Framework for Recruitment and Development**: The competency framework should be integrated into the organization's recruitment processes, ensuring that job descriptions clearly outline the required competencies. During the selection process, candidates should be assessed based on these competencies to determine their fit for the role. Additionally, the framework should guide employee development, with training programs and development plans tailored to address competency gaps.

Example and Case Study

One effective example of a competency framework is that of **Procter & Gamble (P&G)**, which uses the P&G Leadership Competency Model to guide its recruitment, development, and succession planning processes. The model outlines competencies such as **entrepreneurial spirit, influential leadership**, and **personal integrity**. Each competency is broken down into specific behaviours and measurable indicators. For example, under **entrepreneurial spirit**, the behavioural indicators include "demonstrates curiosity and willingness to learn," "drives innovative thinking," and "takes calculated risks." These indicators are used to assess potential leaders during interviews and performance reviews, guiding development through targeted training programs.

Impact on Business

Developing competency frameworks with behavioural indicators provides several benefits:

1. **Enhanced Recruitment and Selection**: By clearly defining what is expected in each role, organizations can more effectively recruit candidates who possess the necessary skills and behaviours. This reduces turnover and ensures that new hires are set up for success.

2. **Targeted Development Plans**: The framework allows for personalized development plans, addressing specific skill gaps and preparing employees for future roles. This targeted approach increases engagement and motivation, leading to higher performance.

3. **Aligned Organizational Goals**: Competency frameworks ensure that all employees, regardless of their role, are working towards the same organizational goals. This alignment improves teamwork, collaboration, and overall business performance.

4. **Succession Planning**: The framework facilitates succession planning by identifying high-potential employees who possess the required competencies for leadership roles, ensuring continuity and stability within the organization.

Final Outcome

By developing robust competency frameworks with behavioural indicators, organizations can create a well-defined pathway for employee growth and development. This not only enhances individual performance but also contributes to a more capable and cohesive workforce, ultimately leading to better business outcomes. It ensures that talent management is proactive rather than reactive, positioning the organization for long-term success in a competitive environment.

A table with basic competencies and their behavioural indicators for **base-level employee**

Competency	Behavioura Indicators
Communication	- Effectively conveys information in both written and verbal formats. - Listens actively and attentively. - Tailors communication style to different audiences. - Clarifies understanding by asking relevant questions.
Problem Solving	- Identifies problems and proposes solutions. - Uses basic analytical skills to analyse data. - Demonstrates creativity in finding solutions. - Considers the impact of decisions on team and organization.
Teamwork	- Collaborates effectively with colleagues. - Contributes to group discussions and decisions. - Shows respect for others' opinions and ideas. - Actively participates in team activities and projects.
Time Management	- Prioritizes tasks based on importance and deadlines. - Manages workload efficiently and meets deadlines. - Avoids procrastination and distractions. - Adapts plans as necessary to accommodate unexpected changes.
Adaptability	- Embraces and adapts to change. - Demonstrates flexibility in work approach. - Takes initiative to learn new skills. - Adjusts quickly to new tools, processes, and environments.
Customer Orientation	- Demonstrates a customer-focused approach. - Addresses customer inquiries and concerns professionally. - Resolves complaints in a timely and effective manner. - Provides accurate information and guidance to customers.
Technical Skills	- Utilizes basic software and tools required for the role. - Demonstrates basic understanding of systems and technology. - Identifies issues with technical systems and seeks appropriate support. - Maintains a focus on accuracy and detail.
Ethical Behaviour	- Acts with integrity and honesty. - Respects company policies and guidelines. - Reports unethical practices or concerns without fear of retaliation. - Adheres to confidentiality standards.
Initiative	- Takes proactive steps to solve problems. - Seeks opportunities for self-improvement and learning. - Takes responsibility for tasks and assignments. - Volunteers for additional responsibilities when needed.

Leadership Potential	- Demonstrates leadership qualities through guidance and mentoring. - Motivates team members and peers. - Takes responsibility for personal and team development. - Leads by example, demonstrating professionalism and commitment to the organization's values.

This table provides a clear set of competencies and specific behavioural indicators for a base-level employee, aligning with the core skills needed for effective performance in a role.

A table with minimum 15 different advanced competencies and their behavioural indicators for **Leadership/CXO Level** employees

Competency	Behavioural Indicators
Strategic Thinking	- Demonstrates the ability to see the big picture and anticipate future trends. - Develops and implements long-term strategies. - Balances short-term goals with long-term objectives. - Integrates diverse viewpoints into decision-making.
Executive Leadership	- Leads with a clear, inspiring vision that aligns with the organization's mission. - Influences and motivates others to achieve shared goals. - Builds and sustains high-performance teams. - Demonstrates resilience and adaptability in crises.
Financial Acumen	- Understands complex financial reports and models. - Makes informed financial decisions to drive business growth. - Manages budgets effectively and allocates resources strategically. - Identifies opportunities for cost optimization and revenue growth.
Decision Making	- Uses data-driven insights to make informed decisions. - Weighs the risks and benefits of different options. - Demonstrates sound judgment in complex situations. - Ensures decisions are consistent with organizational values and goals.
Change Management	- Effectively guides the organization through transformation and change. - Addresses resistance to change with empathy and strategic communication. - Develops and communicates a clear vision of change. - Manages organizational culture shifts.
Stakeholder Engagement	- Builds and maintains strategic relationships with key stakeholders. - Understands the needs and interests of different stakeholders. - Communicates effectively with investors, customers, employees, and external partners.

		- Acts as a liaison between the board, executive team, and stakeholders.
Risk Management		- Identifies, assesses, and mitigates risks to the organization. - Implements robust risk management frameworks. - Monitors and updates risk assessments regularly. - Communicates risk strategies clearly to the board and management.
Innovation Leadership		- Fosters a culture of innovation and creativity within the organization. - Encourages experimentation and calculated risk-taking. - Integrates new technologies and processes to drive competitive advantage. - Drives digital transformation initiatives.
Crisis Management		- Leads the organization through crises with composure and clarity. - Develops crisis management plans and trains the team. - Manages communication during crises to maintain stakeholder trust. - Implements recovery strategies effectively.
Cultural Awareness		- Understands and respects cultural differences in a global marketplace. - Incorporates diversity and inclusion into strategic planning. - Acts as a champion for DEI within the organization. - Ensures global strategies are inclusive and culturally sensitive.
Agility		- Adapts quickly to market changes and shifts in the competitive landscape. - Anticipates future challenges and prepares the organization. - Acts decisively in uncertain environments. - Continuously scans the external environment for emerging trends.
Operational Excellence		- Drives efficiency and process improvement throughout the organization. - Uses data to identify bottlenecks and inefficiencies. - Implements best practices in operations management. - Focuses on quality and consistency in products and services.
Governance & Compliance		- Ensures adherence to regulatory requirements and corporate governance standards. - Implements policies to prevent unethical behaviour. - Conducts regular compliance audits and risk assessments. - Builds a culture of integrity and transparency within the organization.
Leadership Development		- Develops leadership pipelines by identifying high-potential talent. - Coaches and mentors emerging leaders. - Designs leadership development programs aligned with organizational goals. - Fosters a culture of continuous learning and skill development.
Change Communication		- Communicates change initiatives effectively to employees and stakeholders.

| | - Tailors messages to different audiences for clarity and impact.
- Provides regular updates on progress and challenges.
- Encourages feedback and questions during periods of change. |
|---|---|

This table provides a comprehensive list of advanced competencies for Leadership/CXO Level employees, complete with specific behavioural indicators to illustrate effective performance in these roles.

If you are a HR Head – do You think everyone in the Organisation is 10 on 10 on All the Competencies OR there are GAPS which needs to be bridged – through proper Competency Assessment and thereafter taking them through Development Centre to bring them up to levels 3 Competency

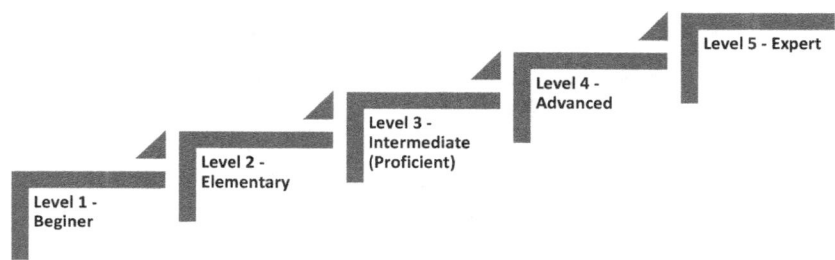

The Role of Mentoring and Coaching for Organizational Success

The role of mentoring and coaching for organizational success is pivotal in fostering growth, enhancing performance, and sustaining a healthy work culture. Both mentoring and coaching provide personalized guidance and support, enabling employees to develop their skills, competencies, and leadership qualities effectively.

Mentoring involves experienced professionals guiding less experienced employees, sharing knowledge, insights, and advice based on their own career journeys and organizational experiences. Mentors help protégés understand the corporate culture, navigate organizational politics, and build relationships with key stakeholders. They also provide valuable perspective on career development, skill enhancement, and leadership development. By aligning mentees' career goals with organizational objectives, mentoring ensures that individuals are not only motivated but also prepared to take on greater responsibilities within the organization. This fosters a sense of loyalty, engagement, and commitment, reducing turnover and increasing employee retention.

Coaching, on the other hand, focuses on enhancing specific skills and behaviors to achieve better performance outcomes. It is more targeted and immediate, often dealing with specific challenges such as improving communication, decision-making, time management, or conflict resolution skills. Coaches work closely with individuals to set goals, identify strengths and weaknesses, and develop strategies for personal and professional development. This process not only helps employees improve their current performance but also prepares them for future leadership roles. Through constructive feedback, goal setting, and action plans, coaching drives the development of competencies critical to leadership effectiveness.

Both mentoring and coaching contribute significantly to organizational success by building a strong leadership pipeline, enhancing organizational agility, and fostering a culture of continuous learning. They help bridge the gap between current and desired performance levels, ensuring that employees at all levels are aligned with the organization's strategic goals. By investing in these development practices, organizations can cultivate a highly skilled and motivated workforce capable of driving innovation, adapting to change, and achieving sustainable growth.

Here are some of the best examples of mentoring and coaching initiatives from organizations and their outcomes:

1. General Electric (GE): Mentoring for Leadership Development

Program: GE has been known for its leadership pipeline and mentoring initiatives under its "Leadership Development Program (LDP)." Senior leaders mentor emerging talents to ensure the development of future leaders with a focus on innovation, strategic thinking, and operational excellence.

Outcome:

- **Result:** GE consistently produced industry-leading executives, many of whom went on to become CEOs at other Fortune 500 companies.
- **Impact:** Strengthened leadership pipeline, increased employee retention, and sustained organizational innovation.

2. Google's Career Mentoring Program

Program: Google offers a robust internal mentoring program where employees are paired with mentors based on their career goals, fostering a culture of learning and development.

Outcome:

- **Result:** Employees reported greater job satisfaction and career clarity.
- **Impact:** Higher retention rates and enhanced employee engagement contributed to Google being consistently ranked as a top employer.

3. Procter & Gamble (P&G): Peer-to-Peer Mentoring

Program: P&G implemented a peer-to-peer mentoring initiative to support cross-functional collaboration and knowledge-sharing. Junior and senior employees collaborate to enhance their technical and leadership skills.

Outcome:

- **Result:** Accelerated the onboarding process and fostered a collaborative work environment.
- **Impact:** Improved innovation and operational efficiency across departments.

4. Microsoft: Executive Coaching for Transformation

Program: Microsoft introduced executive coaching to help senior leaders adapt to Satya Nadella's transformation strategy, focusing on collaboration, empathy, and innovation.

Outcome:

- **Result:** Leaders embraced a growth mindset, leading to cultural transformation.
- **Impact:** Boosted financial performance, with market capitalization increasing from $300 billion in 2014 to over $2 trillion by 2023.

5. Deloitte: Women in Leadership Mentorship Program

Program: Deloitte launched a mentoring program to support women in leadership, offering guidance and sponsorship to advance their careers.

Outcome:

- **Result:** Increased representation of women in senior leadership roles by 30% over five years.
- **Impact:** Fostered diversity, improved organizational culture, and enhanced decision-making.

6. Toyota: Coaching for Operational Excellence

Program: Toyota implements "Kaizen Coaching" to train employees in continuous improvement principles through hands-on guidance and feedback.

Outcome:

- **Result:** Employees demonstrated improved problem-solving skills and implemented over 10,000 process improvements annually.

- **Impact:** Reduced operational costs and enhanced productivity globally.

7. IBM: Reverse Mentoring for Digital Transformation

Program: IBM initiated a reverse mentoring program where younger employees mentored senior executives on emerging technologies and digital tools.
Outcome:

- **Result:** Executives became more digitally savvy, enabling faster adoption of digital transformation strategies.
- **Impact:** Maintained competitive advantage in the tech industry and improved innovation speed.

8. Johnson & Johnson: Leadership Coaching for Global Teams

Program: Johnson & Johnson uses external executive coaches to enhance the leadership skills of their global team leaders, focusing on emotional intelligence, strategic thinking, and cross-cultural communication.
Outcome:

- **Result:** Leaders reported a 40% improvement in team collaboration and decision-making.
- **Impact:** Increased market share in emerging markets and improved global team performance.

9. Starbucks: Manager Coaching for Frontline Staff

Program: Starbucks developed a coaching program for store managers to enhance their ability to mentor frontline staff in customer service and leadership.

Outcome:

- **Result:** Managers developed better communication and leadership skills, improving employee satisfaction scores by 25%.

- **Impact:** Boosted customer loyalty and increased same-store sales globally.

10. Unilever: Mentoring for Sustainable Leadership

Program: Unilever pairs senior leaders with junior employees in sustainability-focused mentoring to embed ESG principles in operations.
Outcome:

- **Result:** Employees reported higher engagement and a deeper understanding of sustainable practices.

- **Impact:** Enhanced Unilever's ESG performance, improving brand reputation and market positioning.

Key Takeaways:

- Mentoring and coaching create lasting impacts by aligning employee development with organizational goals.

- These examples demonstrate improved employee engagement, stronger leadership pipelines, operational efficiency, and enhanced financial performance.

- Companies that prioritize mentoring and coaching also benefit from greater innovation, diversity, and sustainability, ensuring long-term success.

Addressing nepotism and favouritism in Talent Management

Nepotism and favouritism undermine organizational equity, morale, and performance. When promotions or rewards are based on personal connections rather than merit, employees lose trust in the system, leading to resentment, disengagement, and high turnover rates. To address these issues effectively, organizations need structured, transparent, and inclusive talent management processes. Below is an exploration of strategies and case studies addressing nepotism and favouritism in talent management:

1. Implementing Transparent Recruitment Processes

Strategy: Standardized recruitment procedures with clearly defined job descriptions, competency-based assessments, and panel interviews reduce the influence of personal biases.

Example:

- **Company:** Infosys
- **Action:** Infosys developed a rigorous talent acquisition framework, ensuring roles are filled based on technical skills and cultural fit rather than personal referrals.
- **Outcome:** Improved employee trust and reduced bias in hiring decisions.

2. Establishing Objective Performance Metrics

Strategy: Use objective performance indicators like Key Performance Indicators (KPIs) and Balanced Scorecards to evaluate employees based on their contributions rather than subjective preferences.
Example:

- **Company:** General Electric (GE)

- **Action:** GE introduced a transparent appraisal system called "Session C" to assess performance and potential through cross-departmental reviews.
- **Outcome:** Reduced perceptions of favoritism and enhanced career progression clarity.

3. Regular Audits of Talent Management Processes

Strategy: Conduct internal audits to identify patterns of favouritism or nepotism in hiring, promotions, and rewards.

Example:

- **Company:** HSBC
- **Action:** HSBC's HR team conducted biannual reviews of promotion and appraisal data to identify any discrepancies in diversity or fairness.
- **Outcome:** Improved gender and minority representation in leadership roles.

4. Promoting Whistleblower Mechanisms

Strategy: Encourage employees to report instances of nepotism and favouritism through anonymous whistleblowing channels without fear of retaliation.

Example:

- **Company:** Siemens
- **Action:** Siemens launched a secure whistleblowing hotline to address unethical practices, including favouritism in talent management.

- **Outcome:** Strengthened organizational culture and improved ethical decision-making.

5. Leadership Training on Unconscious Bias

Strategy: Train leaders and managers to recognize and mitigate unconscious biases that may lead to favouritism or nepotism.

Example:

- **Company:** Google
- **Action:** Google implemented "Bias-Busting" workshops for managers to promote equitable decision-making in hiring and promotions.
- **Outcome:** Enhanced employee satisfaction and trust in leadership.

6. Leveraging Data Analytics in Talent Management

Strategy: Use data analytics to identify trends and anomalies in recruitment, appraisals, and promotions.

Example:

- **Company:** Netflix
- **Action:** Netflix used analytics to track promotion rates and found that transparent data-sharing improved employee confidence in the fairness of processes.
- **Outcome:** Reduced employee turnover and fostered a high-performance culture.

7. Developing Clear Promotion Guidelines

Strategy: Publish promotion criteria and provide feedback to all employees, ensuring opportunities are based on merit.

Example:

- **Company:** IBM
- **Action:** IBM established transparent career progression pathways with competency maps for each role.
- **Outcome:** Improved employee retention and engagement.

Impact of Addressing Nepotism and Favouritism

- **Employee Engagement:** When employees perceive fairness, their motivation and productivity increase.
- **Retention:** Reduced turnover rates as employees feel valued based on their contributions.
- **Reputation:** Organizations known for equitable talent management attract better talent and earn stakeholders' trust.
- **Performance:** A merit-based culture leads to stronger teams and better organizational outcomes.

Case Study: Eliminating Favouritism at Tata Steel

- **Issue:** Tata Steel faced allegations of favouritism in internal promotions, leading to employee dissatisfaction.
- **Action:** The company implemented a 360-degree feedback system and tied promotions to measurable KPIs.
- **Outcome:** Employee trust in the management improved, resulting in increased retention rates and enhanced productivity.

By implementing these strategies and maintaining transparency, organizations can build a culture of trust, fairness, and excellence, driving long-term sustainability and success.

Chapter 6: The Role of Leadership in Ethical Management

How CEOs and top management influence culture and sustainability

Choosing and training CEOs: Building a new competency model

Transitioning from functional leadership to organizational leadership

The Role of Leadership in Ethical Management

Leadership plays a pivotal role in fostering ethical management, shaping organizational culture, and ensuring long-term success. Ethical leadership sets the tone for integrity, fairness, and accountability, impacting decision-making processes, stakeholder relationships, and overall business sustainability. Below are key roles that leaders play in promoting ethical management, supported by examples and outcomes.

1. Setting Ethical Standards

Leaders establish and communicate a clear code of ethics, ensuring it aligns with organizational goals and values. By modelling ethical behaviour, leaders influence employees to follow suit.

Example:

- **Company:** Johnson & Johnson
- **Action:** During the Tylenol crisis in 1982, CEO James Burke prioritized customer safety over profit by recalling 31 million bottles of Tylenol, costing the company $100 million.
- **Outcome:** This ethical decision preserved the company's reputation and restored consumer trust.

2. Driving Accountability

Ethical leaders hold themselves and their teams accountable for their actions. They encourage transparency in reporting and decision-making to prevent unethical practices like data manipulation or favouritism.

Example:

- **Company:** Patagonia
- **Action:** CEO Rose Marcario emphasized accountability by ensuring sustainable practices across the supply chain, even at higher costs.
- **Outcome:** Patagonia gained consumer loyalty and reinforced its brand as an ethical leader in environmental sustainability.

---

3. Encouraging Open Communication

Ethical leaders create safe environments for employees to voice concerns about unethical behaviour without fear of retaliation. They establish whistleblowing channels and respond promptly to address issues.

Example:

- **Company:** Siemens
- **Action:** Siemens launched an internal compliance program after its 2008 bribery scandal, emphasizing open communication and whistleblower protections.
- **Outcome:** Improved ethical practices and regained stakeholder trust.

---

4. Promoting Fairness and Equity

Leaders ensure equal opportunities for employees, focusing on merit-based decision-making in hiring, promotions, and rewards. They actively work to eliminate nepotism and unconscious bias.

Example:

- **Company:** Microsoft

- **Action:** Under Satya Nadella's leadership, Microsoft introduced programs to promote diversity, equity, and inclusion (DEI), tying leadership bonuses to DEI goals.
- **Outcome:** Enhanced workplace inclusivity and strengthened employee engagement.

5. Leading by Example

Ethical leaders demonstrate integrity in their daily actions, setting an example for employees to emulate. Their decisions prioritize long-term sustainability over short-term gains.

Example:

- **Company:** Unilever
- **Action:** CEO Paul Polman refused to provide quarterly financial guidance, focusing instead on sustainable growth and ethical practices.
- **Outcome:** Unilever achieved consistent growth and strengthened its reputation as a sustainability leader.

6. Embedding Ethics into Organizational Strategy

Leaders integrate ethical considerations into strategic planning, aligning business goals with societal and environmental responsibilities.

Example:

- **Company:** Starbucks
- **Action:** CEO Kevin Johnson committed to sustainability by setting ambitious goals to reduce carbon emissions and waste.
- **Outcome:** Strengthened brand image and customer loyalty, contributing to financial success.

Impact of Ethical Leadership

1. **For Employees:**
    - Increases morale, trust, and job satisfaction.
    - Reduces turnover rates and enhances productivity.
2. **For Customers:**
    - Builds brand loyalty and trust in the organization.
3. **For Shareholders:**
    - Ensures long-term profitability and sustainable growth.
4. **For Society:**
    - Promotes positive social and environmental impacts.
5. **For the Organization:**
    - Strengthens reputation, reduces legal risks, and fosters innovation.

Case Study: Ethical Leadership at Tesla

- **Issue:** Tesla faced criticism for labor practices and customer service under its rapid expansion.
- **Action:** Elon Musk addressed these concerns by increasing transparency, ensuring workers' rights, and improving customer engagement through direct communication.
- **Outcome:** Despite challenges, Tesla maintained a strong brand presence and continued to innovate, reflecting a commitment to ethical management.

Ethical leadership is not just a moral imperative; it is a strategic necessity for organizations aiming to thrive in a competitive, socially conscious world.

Leaders who prioritize ethics create resilient, successful businesses that benefit all stakeholders.

How CEOs and Top Management influence Culture and Sustainability

CEOs and top management have a profound impact on shaping organizational culture and embedding sustainability into business operations. Their decisions, behaviours, and leadership styles set the tone for ethical practices, long-term strategic planning, and environmental and social responsibility. Below are key areas where their influence is pivotal, supported by examples and case studies.

1. Shaping Organizational Culture

The CEO and top management establish core values that define the workplace environment, decision-making processes, and employee behaviours. By demonstrating a commitment to ethics, inclusivity, and innovation, they set a standard for the entire organization.

Example:

- **Company:** Microsoft
- **Action:** Under Satya Nadella's leadership, the company shifted from a "know-it-all" to a "learn-it-all" culture. He emphasized empathy, collaboration, and growth mindset across teams.
- **Outcome:** This cultural shift improved employee morale, enhanced innovation, and revitalized Microsoft's global market position.

2. Driving Sustainability Goals

Top management integrates sustainability into business strategies by setting measurable environmental, social, and governance (ESG) goals. They allocate resources to achieve these objectives and ensure alignment with global standards like the UN Sustainable Development Goals (SDGs).

Example:

- **Company:** IKEA
- **Action:** CEO Jesper Brodin committed to making IKEA a circular business by 2030, focusing on renewable energy, sustainable sourcing, and waste reduction.
- **Outcome:** IKEA achieved significant progress in reducing its carbon footprint, enhancing brand reputation, and attracting environmentally conscious customers.

3. Role Modelling Ethical Leadership

CEOs influence culture and sustainability by embodying ethical leadership. Their actions—such as promoting transparency, taking accountability, and addressing unethical practices—directly impact employee behaviours and stakeholder trust.

Example:

- **Company:** Patagonia
- **Action:** Yvon Chouinard, founder and former CEO, embedded environmental responsibility into Patagonia's DNA. He emphasized ethical sourcing, fair trade, and advocacy for climate action.
- **Outcome:** Patagonia became a leader in corporate social responsibility, inspiring loyalty among employees and customers alike.

4. Fostering Innovation for Sustainability

Top management champions innovation by investing in technologies and processes that drive sustainability. Their decisions to adopt green technologies or rethink supply chains demonstrate their commitment to a sustainable future.

Example:

- **Company:** Tesla
- **Action:** Elon Musk prioritized electric vehicles and renewable energy solutions, challenging traditional automotive models.
- **Outcome:** Tesla transformed the automotive industry and solidified its role as a leader in sustainable innovation.

5. Building Stakeholder Engagement

CEOs actively engage stakeholders—employees, investors, customers, and communities—to foster a shared vision of sustainability. Transparent communication and collaborative initiatives ensure widespread buy-in and long-term success.

Example:

- **Company:** Unilever
- **Action:** Under Paul Polman's leadership, Unilever launched the Sustainable Living Plan, engaging employees and suppliers to achieve sustainability goals.
- **Outcome:** The company reduced environmental impact and increased market share in sustainable product categories.

6. Setting the Governance Framework

Top management ensures robust governance mechanisms to monitor and evaluate sustainability and cultural initiatives. This includes policies, metrics, and regular audits to maintain accountability.

Example:

- **Company:** Danone
- **Action:** CEO Emmanuel Faber implemented a governance model that integrated sustainability into financial reporting and decision-making.
- **Outcome:** Danone achieved B Corp certification, reinforcing its reputation as a purpose-driven organization.

Impact of CEO and Top Management Influence

1. **For Employees:**
    - Promotes a sense of purpose, improving job satisfaction and retention.
    - Encourages ethical behaviours and alignment with organizational values.

2. **For Customers:**
    - Builds trust and loyalty by aligning business practices with consumer values.

3. **For Investors:**
    - Demonstrates commitment to long-term growth and risk mitigation through sustainable practices.

4. **For Society and the Environment:**
    - Contributes to global sustainability goals and fosters positive societal impact.

5. **For the Organization:**
    - Enhances resilience, profitability, and market differentiation.

Case Study: Salesforce

- **CEO Influence:** Marc Benioff has been instrumental in creating a culture of equality and sustainability at Salesforce.

- **Actions:** Introduced pay equity initiatives, integrated philanthropy through the 1-1-1 model, and committed to achieving net-zero emissions.

- **Outcomes:** Salesforce experienced increased employee engagement, strong customer loyalty, and enhanced financial performance while contributing to social and environmental causes.

CEOs and top management hold the power to transform organizations into ethical and sustainable entities. By embedding culture and sustainability into their leadership approach, they ensure long-term success while positively impacting society and the environment.

Choosing and Training CEOs: Building a new Competency Model

The role of a CEO is no longer limited to overseeing financial performance or operational efficiency. Modern CEOs must navigate a rapidly changing business landscape marked by technological disruption, globalization, social responsibility, and environmental challenges. To prepare future leaders, organizations must develop a **new competency model** tailored to these demands. This model emphasizes a blend of technical, interpersonal, and strategic skills, along with the ability to drive innovation, manage risks, and foster a sustainable and ethical culture.

Core Components of the New CEO Competency Model

1. Strategic Vision and Execution

A successful CEO must possess a clear vision for the organization's future and the ability to translate it into actionable plans.

- **Competencies:** Long-term planning, strategic agility, resource allocation.
- **Training Methods:** Scenario planning workshops, strategic simulations, and exposure to cross-industry trends.

Example:

- **Sundar Pichai (Google):** Demonstrated strategic foresight by focusing on AI and cloud technologies, positioning Google as a leader in innovation.

---

2. Emotional Intelligence (EQ)

Modern CEOs must navigate complex interpersonal dynamics and lead diverse teams. High emotional intelligence is critical for effective communication, conflict resolution, and empathy.

- **Competencies:** Self-awareness, empathy, relationship management.
- **Training Methods:** Executive coaching, 360-degree feedback, and leadership retreats.

Example:

- **Mary Barra (GM):** Her empathetic leadership helped steer General Motors through cultural transformation and innovation.

---

3. Ethical Decision-Making

CEOs are responsible for upholding organizational integrity. Ethical decision-making ensures trust with stakeholders and aligns with societal values.

- **Competencies:** Transparency, accountability, adherence to ESG principles.

- **Training Methods:** Case studies on ethical dilemmas, simulations, and governance workshops.

Example:

- **Paul Polman (Unilever):** Integrated sustainability into business strategy, making ethical decisions a cornerstone of corporate success.

4. Innovation and Adaptability

The ability to adapt to disruptive changes and foster a culture of innovation is essential for modern CEOs.

- **Competencies:** Technology acumen, design thinking, risk-taking.
- **Training Methods:** Digital transformation courses, innovation labs, and exposure to startups.

Example:

- **Satya Nadella (Microsoft):** Transformed Microsoft by adopting a growth mindset and focusing on cloud computing and AI.

5. Global and Cultural Awareness

CEOs must operate across borders, understanding global markets, cultural diversity, and geopolitical challenges.

- **Competencies:** Cross-cultural communication, geopolitical insight, stakeholder engagement.
- **Training Methods:** International rotations, diversity training, and partnerships with global organizations.

Example:

- **Indra Nooyi (PepsiCo):** Advocated for diversity and inclusion while expanding PepsiCo's global footprint.

6. Sustainability Leadership

Modern CEOs must champion sustainability initiatives and align them with business objectives.

- **Competencies:** Environmental stewardship, ESG alignment, circular economy practices.
- **Training Methods:** Sustainability workshops, partnerships with environmental organizations, and ESG reporting training.

Example:

- **Jesper Brodin (IKEA):** Committed to circular business practices and renewable energy adoption.

---

7. Crisis Management and Resilience

CEOs must handle crises effectively, maintaining calm and steering the organization toward recovery.

- **Competencies:** Decision-making under pressure, resilience, stakeholder communication.
- **Training Methods:** Crisis simulations, media training, and resilience-building programs.

Example:

- **Brian Chesky (Airbnb):** Successfully navigated the COVID-19 crisis by pivoting the business model and rebuilding trust with stakeholders.

Training Framework for Future CEOs

To develop these competencies, organizations should implement a robust training framework:

1. **Experiential Learning:** On-the-job assignments, leadership shadowing, and cross-functional roles.
2. **Coaching and Mentoring:** Regular sessions with seasoned leaders and industry experts.
3. **Continuous Education:** Enrolment in executive education programs focused on emerging trends.
4. **Feedback Mechanisms:** Regular 360-degree feedback to refine leadership style.
5. **Technology Integration:** Use of AI-driven leadership development tools for personalized learning paths.

Case Study: IBM's Leadership Development Program

IBM identified leadership as a critical component of its transformation strategy and created a structured program to groom future CEOs.

- **Components:**
    - Rotational assignments in key markets.
    - Exposure to emerging technologies like AI and blockchain.
    - Coaching from senior executives.
- **Outcome:** Enabled leaders like Ginni Rometty to drive innovation and cultural transformation, solidifying IBM's competitive edge.

Impact of the New Competency Model

1. **For Organizations:**
    - Increased agility and resilience in volatile markets.

o   Improved stakeholder trust and brand reputation.

2. **For Shareholders:**

   o   Sustainable growth and long-term profitability.

3. **For Employees:**

   o   Enhanced workplace culture and alignment with leadership values.

4. **For Society and Environment:**

   o   Stronger commitment to ESG goals and community impact.

This competency model ensures that future CEOs are not just business leaders but also visionaries, innovators, and ethical stewards, capable of driving sustainable success in a complex and dynamic world.

Transitioning from Functional Leadership to Organizational Leadership

The journey from functional leadership—managing a specific department or function—to organizational leadership, where one oversees the entire enterprise, is a significant transition. It requires a shift in perspective, skill set, and responsibilities, as leaders move from focusing on operational excellence to aligning strategic goals across the organization.

Key Differences Between Functional and Organizational Leadership

Aspect	Functional Leadership	Organizational Leadership
Scope of Influence	Limited to a department or function.	Encompasses the entire organization.
Focus	Operational efficiency and departmental goals.	Vision, strategy, and alignment of organizational goals.
Decision-Making	Tactical and function-specific.	Strategic and enterprise-wide.
Perspective	Short to medium-term planning.	Long-term planning and sustainability.

| Stakeholder Engagement | Limited to team members and department-related stakeholders. | Broad, including investors, customers, employees, and society. |

Key Competencies for Organizational Leadership

1. Strategic Thinking

Leaders must develop the ability to envision the future of the organization, identify opportunities, and navigate uncertainties.

- **Shift Required:** From focusing on team goals to driving organizational strategy.
- **Example:** Transitioning from managing marketing campaigns to aligning marketing efforts with broader business objectives, like entering new markets.

2. Cross-Functional Collaboration

Organizational leaders need to work across departments, breaking silos to ensure cohesion and shared vision.

- **Shift Required:** From managing within a function to fostering collaboration across multiple functions.
- **Example:** A CFO working closely with HR and Operations to manage post-merger integration effectively.

3. Broader Accountability

Leadership now involves responsibility for overall organizational success, including financial performance, culture, and reputation.

- **Shift Required:** From being accountable for a department's KPIs to owning the organization's outcomes.

- **Example:** An R&D head transitioning to CEO must balance innovation investments with financial prudence and shareholder expectations.

4. Visionary Communication

Organizational leaders must inspire and align diverse teams and stakeholders.

- **Shift Required:** From communicating within teams to articulating vision across the organization and beyond.
- **Example:** Satya Nadella, during his transition to Microsoft CEO, successfully communicated a growth mindset and cultural transformation strategy.

Challenges in Transitioning

1. **Letting Go of Operational Control**
    - Functional leaders often struggle to delegate operational tasks as they shift focus to strategy.
    - **Solution:** Develop trust in middle management and adopt delegation frameworks.

2. **Developing a Broader Perspective**
    - Leaders must understand how different functions contribute to organizational goals.
    - **Solution:** Engage in cross-functional projects and leadership rotations.

3. **Building Influence at Scale**
    - Engaging with a wide array of stakeholders requires enhanced interpersonal and negotiation skills.

- **Solution:** Participate in coaching programs and stakeholder engagement workshops.

Case Studies of Successful Transitions

1. Indra Nooyi (PepsiCo)

Transitioned from leading corporate strategy to CEO. She integrated sustainability into PepsiCo's business model, focusing on long-term growth.

- **Outcome:** Achieved significant revenue growth while fostering a culture of innovation and inclusivity.

2. Andy Jassy (Amazon)

Transitioned from leading AWS (Amazon Web Services) to becoming Amazon's CEO. Jassy brought his expertise in scaling AWS to the broader organization.

- **Outcome:** Sustained Amazon's growth trajectory by expanding e-commerce and cloud operations.

3. Marillyn Hewson (Lockheed Martin)

From managing specific business segments to CEO, Hewson focused on innovation and global market expansion.

- **Outcome:** Enhanced Lockheed Martin's position as a leader in defense and aerospace.

Best Practices for Transitioning

1. **Gain a Holistic View of the Business**
   - Participate in cross-functional leadership forums and strategy sessions.
   - **Example:** Leadership rotations across functions, such as moving from operations to marketing or finance.

2. **Invest in Leadership Development Programs**
    - Attend courses focusing on strategic leadership, vision building, and stakeholder management.
    - **Example:** IBM's Global Leadership Development Program trains potential leaders in innovation and strategy.

3. **Focus on Cultural Alignment**
    - Emphasize cultural change and shared values as part of the transition.
    - **Example:** Microsoft's cultural transformation under Satya Nadella, focusing on collaboration and growth mindset.

Final Outcome of a Successful Transition

A leader who successfully transitions to organizational leadership becomes a catalyst for growth, innovation, and alignment. They empower teams, build a sustainable culture, and drive the organization toward achieving long-term goals, ensuring success across all dimensions—financial, operational, and societal.

Chapter 7: Governance and ESG Integration

Aligning management practices with ESG principles

Sustainable decision-making for long-term profitability

Creating governance frameworks to ensure ethical leadership

Governance and ESG Integration

Governance plays a critical role in effectively integrating Environmental, Social, and Governance (ESG) principles into an organization's strategy. Strong governance ensures transparency, accountability, and ethical decision-making, enabling the organization to achieve its ESG goals while fostering trust among stakeholders.

Core Components of Governance in ESG Integration

1. **Board Oversight and Accountability**
    - Boards must actively oversee ESG initiatives, aligning them with the organization's vision and strategy.
    - **Example:** Unilever's Board ESG Committee ensures sustainability initiatives align with their corporate goals, fostering long-term value creation.

2. **Ethical Leadership**
    - Leadership must embody ethical practices, fostering a culture that prioritizes ESG considerations.
    - **Example:** Patagonia's leadership prioritizes environmental sustainability, embedding it into all aspects of their business operations.

3. **Risk Management**
    - Identifying and managing ESG-related risks, such as climate change impacts or human rights issues, is essential.
    - **Example:** BlackRock incorporates climate risk into its investment decisions, requiring portfolio companies to disclose sustainability practices.

4. **Stakeholder Engagement**
    - Governance frameworks should include mechanisms for engaging employees, investors, customers, and communities in ESG dialogues.
    - **Example:** IKEA engages stakeholders through its People & Planet Positive strategy, aiming for a circular and climate-positive business by 2030.

5. **Transparency and Reporting**
    - Organizations should adopt global standards like GRI, SASB, or TCFD to report ESG performance, ensuring credibility and comparability.
    - **Example:** Microsoft transparently reports progress toward its carbon-negative commitment using science-based targets.

Steps to Integrate ESG Through Governance

1. **Incorporating ESG Metrics into KPIs**
    - Link executive compensation and performance reviews to ESG outcomes.
    - **Case Study:** Danone ties 20% of its executives' bonuses to the company's sustainability goals, fostering alignment across leadership.

2. **Developing ESG Policies and Codes of Conduct**
   - Establish clear ESG policies, ensuring compliance across the organization and its value chain.
   - **Example:** Apple has a Supplier Code of Conduct to ensure ethical sourcing of materials, particularly rare earth minerals.

3. **Training and Capacity Building**
   - Train board members and executives on ESG trends, risks, and opportunities.
   - **Example:** Nestlé offers ESG-specific training to its leadership, ensuring informed decision-making at the highest levels.

4. **Fostering ESG Data Governance**
   - Ensure accurate, consistent, and transparent ESG data collection and reporting processes.
   - **Example:** Walmart uses AI-driven analytics to track its sustainability metrics, improving accuracy and decision-making.

Challenges in Governance for ESG Integration

1. **Balancing Short-term and Long-term Goals**
   - Pressure for immediate financial returns can conflict with long-term ESG objectives.

2. **Complex Regulatory Environments**
   - Navigating different ESG-related regulations across regions can complicate governance frameworks.

3. **Data Integrity Issues**

- Ensuring reliable ESG data for decision-making and reporting remains a significant challenge.

Benefits of Strong Governance in ESG

1. **Enhanced Stakeholder Trust**
   - Transparent governance fosters trust among investors, employees, and customers.
   - **Statistical Insight:** According to Edelman's Trust Barometer, 88% of investors prioritize transparency in ESG reporting.

2. **Improved Financial Performance**
   - Companies with robust ESG governance often outperform peers financially.
   - **Example:** A 2022 MSCI study found ESG-focused companies had 20% higher return on equity.

3. **Risk Mitigation**
   - Addressing ESG risks proactively protects the organization from reputational and financial harm.
   - **Example:** Companies with climate risk strategies, like Tesla, are better prepared for regulatory changes in emissions.

4. **Attracting and Retaining Talent**
   - Employees prefer working for companies with strong ESG commitments.
   - **Statistical Insight:** A Glassdoor survey revealed 75% of employees expect their employer to prioritize sustainability.

Case Study: Governance and ESG Integration at Starbucks

Problem: Starbucks faced criticism for unsustainable sourcing practices and waste management issues.

Action Taken:

- Established a dedicated ESG committee under its board of directors.
- Introduced ethical sourcing guidelines for coffee and other raw materials.
- Set sustainability goals, including reducing carbon emissions and water usage by 50% by 2030.

Outcome:

- Increased customer loyalty and employee satisfaction.
- Enhanced reputation as a sustainable and ethical brand.
- Financial growth attributed to responsible sourcing and waste reduction strategies.

Conclusion

Governance acts as the backbone for ESG integration, ensuring that sustainability and ethical practices are embedded into the organization's DNA. By prioritizing transparency, stakeholder engagement, and strategic alignment, companies can create a resilient and responsible business model that delivers long-term value for all stakeholders.

No Manipulation on ESG Data

Governance and ESG Integration Without Manipulation

Governance forms the backbone of effective ESG (Environmental, Social, and Governance) integration, ensuring that sustainability initiatives are genuine, measurable, and aligned with long-term business goals. By avoiding manipulative practices like greenwashing, selective reporting, or data manipulation, organizations build trust with stakeholders and secure sustainable growth.

Key Pillars of Authentic ESG Integration

1. Transparent Reporting

- **What It Means:** Honest disclosure of ESG data and performance metrics, including Scope 1, 2, and 3 emissions.
- **Example:** Unilever's transparent reporting of emissions across its entire supply chain, verified by third-party audits.
- **Impact:** Strengthened investor confidence and increased brand loyalty due to consistent sustainability achievements.

2. Independent Audits and Verification

- **What It Means:** Engaging third-party organizations to verify ESG claims and data.
- **Example:** Patagonia's environmental initiatives undergo regular audits by B Corp to ensure compliance with sustainability standards.
- **Impact:** Enhanced credibility among customers and investors, reinforcing Patagonia's reputation as a leader in ethical business practices.

3. Leadership Accountability

- **What It Means:** Boards and executives taking direct responsibility for ESG performance, with KPIs tied to compensation.

- **Example:** Microsoft's executive bonuses are partially tied to sustainability milestones, including achieving net-zero operations.
- **Impact:** Aligns leadership incentives with organizational sustainability goals, fostering accountability.

4. Materiality Assessment

- **What It Means:** Identifying ESG issues most relevant to the organization and its stakeholders to avoid superficial efforts.
- **Example:** IKEA focuses on sustainable sourcing and renewable energy in alignment with its materiality assessment.
- **Impact:** Maximized impact on environmental and social dimensions while addressing key stakeholder concerns.

Avoiding Manipulation in ESG Practices

Greenwashing

- **Definition:** Misleading stakeholders about the environmental impact of products or practices.
- **Real Example:** H&M faced criticism for labelling garments as "sustainable" without sufficient evidence, resulting in loss of customer trust.
- **Solution:** Clear labelling backed by lifecycle analyses and certifications like GOTS (Global Organic Textile Standard).

Scope 1, 2, and 3 Emissions Misreporting

- **Definition:** Underreporting indirect emissions (Scope 3) to inflate ESG performance.
- **Real Example:** Oil and gas companies often face scrutiny for omitting significant Scope 3 emissions from their reports.

- **Solution:** Adopting frameworks like GHG Protocol for comprehensive and accurate emissions reporting.

Data Manipulation

- **Definition:** Altering metrics to present an inflated or inaccurate ESG performance.
- **Real Example:** Wells Fargo's false account scandal highlighted how manipulation can damage trust across financial and social dimensions.
- **Solution:** Implementing robust governance structures and fostering a culture of integrity in data reporting.

Case Studies: Organizations That Integrate ESG Ethically

1. Danone

- **What They Did:** Danone became the first listed company to adopt the French "Entreprise à Mission" legal framework, focusing on social and environmental impact alongside profitability.
- **Outcome:** Consistent stakeholder trust, increased investment from ESG-focused funds, and steady financial performance.

2. Salesforce

- **What They Did:** Integrated ESG principles into their core operations, focusing on net-zero emissions and social responsibility. ESG performance is audited and transparently reported annually.
- **Outcome:** Secured its position as a technology leader while aligning with global sustainability goals.

3. Neste

- **What They Did:** Focused on renewable energy and sustainable aviation fuels, backed by transparent reporting and third-party verification.

- **Outcome:** Achieved significant growth in green energy markets, strengthening its global reputation.

Tools and Frameworks for Ethical ESG Integration

- **Global Reporting Initiative (GRI):** Ensures standardized, transparent reporting on ESG metrics.
- **Task Force on Climate-Related Financial Disclosures (TCFD):** Guides climate-related financial risk disclosures.
- **ISO 14064:** Standard for measuring and reporting greenhouse gas emissions.
- **Sustainability Accounting Standards Board (SASB):** Aligns ESG metrics with financial materiality.

Final Impact of Ethical ESG Integration

Organizations that integrate ESG without manipulation achieve long-term benefits, including:

- **Increased Shareholder Value:** Ethical ESG practices attract sustainable investments.
- **Enhanced Customer Loyalty:** Transparency fosters trust and brand loyalty.
- **Regulatory Compliance:** Avoid fines and reputational damage by adhering to global standards.
- **Talent Retention:** Employees are drawn to companies that align with their values.
- **Societal Contribution:** Genuine efforts contribute to environmental sustainability and social equity.

By embedding governance into the ESG process and committing to authenticity, organizations not only avoid manipulation but also secure a competitive edge in a rapidly evolving global market.

Aligning management practices with ESG Principles

Aligning management practices with Environmental, Social, and Governance (ESG) principles is essential for organizations aiming to thrive in a rapidly evolving global marketplace. This alignment fosters sustainability, stakeholder trust, and long-term profitability while addressing environmental and social challenges. Here's how management practices can be effectively aligned with ESG principles:

1. Integration into Corporate Strategy

What It Means: ESG principles must be embedded in the core business strategy rather than treated as standalone initiatives.

Example:

- **Company:** Unilever
- **What They Did:** Integrated the "Sustainable Living Plan" into their corporate strategy, focusing on reducing environmental footprint and improving social impact.
- **Outcome:** Achieved cost savings through energy efficiency, increased consumer loyalty, and enhanced brand value.

2. Stakeholder Engagement

What It Means: Regularly engaging stakeholders, including employees, customers, investors, and communities, to align management decisions with ESG expectations.

Example:

- **Company:** Starbucks

- **What They Did:** Engaged with farmers, suppliers, and consumers to create sustainable supply chains and ethical sourcing policies.
- **Outcome:** Improved supply chain resilience and brand reputation among environmentally conscious consumers.

3. Governance Reforms

What It Means: Establishing robust governance frameworks to ensure accountability and transparency in ESG performance.
Example:

- **Company:** Tesla
- **What They Did:** Appointed a dedicated board committee to oversee ESG initiatives, ensuring alignment with business goals.
- **Outcome:** Strengthened investor confidence and met regulatory expectations.

4. Operational Sustainability

What It Means: Implementing practices that reduce waste, conserve resources, and lower carbon emissions.
Example:

- **Company:** IKEA
- **What They Did:** Transitioned to 100% renewable energy and circular design principles in product manufacturing.
- **Outcome:** Reduced environmental impact while lowering operational costs and creating a sustainable supply chain.

5. Employee-Centric Policies

What It Means: Creating an inclusive, equitable, and safe workplace.
Example:

- **Company:** Salesforce
- **What They Did:** Launched programs promoting gender pay equality and workplace diversity.
- **Outcome:** Attracted and retained top talent while improving employee satisfaction and productivity.

6. Data-Driven ESG Metrics

What It Means: Using reliable, measurable metrics to assess and report ESG performance.
Example:

- **Company:** Microsoft
- **What They Did:** Invested in AI and analytics tools to measure Scope 1, 2, and 3 emissions, providing stakeholders with transparent data.
- **Outcome:** Enhanced trust among investors and aligned operations with climate goals.

7. Circular Economy and Innovation

What It Means: Encouraging innovative solutions and circular economy principles to achieve sustainability.

Example:

- **Company:** Adidas
- **What They Did:** Created the "Futurecraft Loop" project to develop fully recyclable running shoes.
- **Outcome:** Established a competitive edge in sustainable fashion while aligning with consumer demand for eco-friendly products.

Case Studies: Success Through ESG-Aligned Management

1. Patagonia

- **What They Did:** Committed to environmental preservation by donating 1% of sales to environmental causes and adopting sustainable manufacturing practices.
- **Impact:** Built a loyal customer base, increased market share, and inspired other businesses to adopt ESG principles.

2. Nestlé

- **What They Did:** Focused on reducing water usage, improving supplier practices, and enhancing community health.
- **Impact:** Achieved cost savings through efficient resource use and strengthened supplier relationships, boosting brand value.

3. Danone

- **What They Did:** Adopted a "B Corp" framework to ensure its business operations and governance met high social and environmental standards.
- **Impact:** Increased stakeholder trust and long-term profitability.

Impact of ESG-Aligned Management Practices

1. **For Shareholders:** Improved ESG performance attracts sustainable investments, boosts market valuation, and mitigates financial risks.
2. **For Employees:** Enhances job satisfaction and retention by fostering an inclusive and purpose-driven work environment.
3. **For Customers:** Builds trust and loyalty among consumers who value ethical and sustainable practices.

4. **For Society and the Environment:** Contributes to global goals like climate action and social equity, creating a positive societal impact.

By aligning management practices with ESG principles, companies ensure they remain competitive while making meaningful contributions to the environment and society. This alignment also secures long-term value for all stakeholders and mitigates risks associated with unethical practices or regulatory non-compliance.

Sustainable Decision-Making for Long-Term Profitability

Sustainable decision-making integrates environmental, social, and governance (ESG) considerations into a company's strategic and operational choices. This approach focuses on creating value for all stakeholders—shareholders, employees, customers, and society—while ensuring long-term profitability and resilience. Here's how sustainable decision-making drives profitability:

1. Resource Efficiency and Cost Savings

Sustainable practices often lead to improved resource efficiency, reducing waste and operational costs.

Example:

- **Company:** General Electric (GE)

- **What They Did:** Implemented the "Ecomagination" initiative, focusing on sustainable innovation and energy-efficient products.

- **Outcome:** Generated $232 billion in revenue since the program's inception, while reducing operational costs and emissions.

2. Market Differentiation and Consumer Loyalty

Sustainability attracts environmentally and socially conscious consumers, enhancing market share and brand value.

Example:

- **Company:** Tesla
- **What They Did:** Focused on electric vehicles (EVs) as a sustainable alternative to internal combustion engine cars.
- **Outcome:** Tesla became a market leader in the EV sector, with a $1 trillion valuation in 2021.

3. Attracting and Retaining Talent

Employees prefer working for organizations committed to sustainability and ethical practices.

Example:

- **Company:** Salesforce
- **What They Did:** Embedded sustainability in its core values, achieving net-zero emissions and 100% renewable energy usage.
- **Outcome:** Attracted top talent and maintained a high employee retention rate, enhancing organizational productivity.

4. Risk Mitigation and Regulatory Compliance

Sustainable decision-making minimizes risks related to regulatory non-compliance, supply chain disruptions, and reputational damage.

Example:

- **Company:** Unilever

- **What They Did:** Adopted sustainable sourcing practices and improved supplier accountability.
- **Outcome:** Reduced supply chain risks while building a reputation as a sustainability leader, attracting ESG-focused investors.

5. Innovation and Competitive Advantage

Sustainability drives innovation, enabling companies to develop new products, services, and business models.

Example:

- **Company:** Adidas
- **What They Did:** Developed eco-friendly products, such as sneakers made from recycled ocean plastic.
- **Outcome:** Strengthened market position and appealed to environmentally conscious consumers.

Case Studies: Long-Term Profitability Through Sustainability

1. IKEA

- **Sustainability Action:** Transitioned to renewable energy and circular economy principles, aiming for a fully circular business model by 2030.
- **Impact:** Achieved cost savings through resource efficiency and strengthened customer loyalty, driving long-term profitability.

2. Nestlé

- **Sustainability Action:** Invested in sustainable water and agricultural practices across its supply chain.
- **Impact:** Reduced environmental risks and enhanced brand trust, contributing to consistent revenue growth.

3. Microsoft

- **Sustainability Action:** Committed to becoming carbon negative by 2030, implementing advanced carbon accounting and sustainable operations.
- **Impact:** Boosted investor confidence and differentiated itself in the tech sector, enhancing shareholder value.

Key Principles for Sustainable Decision-Making

1. **Long-Term Vision:** Focus on strategies that balance short-term financial gains with long-term environmental and social benefits.
2. **Stakeholder Involvement:** Collaborate with shareholders, employees, communities, and governments to align decisions with broader sustainability goals.
3. **Transparent Reporting:** Use robust metrics to track and disclose ESG performance, building stakeholder trust.
4. **Continuous Improvement:** Regularly evaluate and adapt sustainability practices to meet evolving challenges and opportunities.

Benefits of Sustainable Decision-Making

1. **For Shareholders:** Higher returns through risk mitigation and access to ESG-focused investment funds.
2. **For Customers:** Enhanced trust and loyalty due to ethical and sustainable business practices.
3. **For Employees:** Improved job satisfaction and productivity in a purpose-driven workplace.
4. **For Society:** Positive contributions to global sustainability goals, including climate action and social equity.

Sustainable decision-making is no longer optional—it is a business imperative. Companies that embed sustainability into their decision-making processes not only secure long-term profitability but also position themselves as leaders in a rapidly changing global economy.

Creating Governance Frameworks to ensure Ethical Leadership

Governance frameworks provide the structure and principles necessary to promote ethical leadership and foster a culture of accountability, transparency, and integrity. An effective governance framework ensures that leadership decisions align with the organization's core values, legal requirements, and stakeholder expectations. Here's a detailed approach to building such frameworks, supported by examples and case studies.

Key Elements of an Ethical Governance Framework

1. **Code of Ethics and Conduct**

    - Clearly outline the organization's ethical principles, expectations, and behavioural standards.
    - **Example:** Johnson & Johnson's *Credo* emphasizes responsibility to customers, employees, and communities, guiding ethical decision-making for over 75 years.

2. **Board Oversight and Accountability**

    - Establish a diverse, independent board to oversee executive decisions and ensure alignment with ethical goals.
    - **Case Study:** Unilever's board actively monitors the company's sustainability strategy, reinforcing ethical practices across global operations.

3. **Risk Management and Compliance Systems**

- Implement systems to identify, assess, and mitigate risks related to unethical practices or non-compliance.
- **Example:** Microsoft uses AI-driven compliance tools to detect potential violations of its ethical policies.

4. **Whistleblowing Mechanisms**
    - Create anonymous channels for reporting unethical behaviour without fear of retaliation.
    - **Case Study:** Siemens introduced a global whistleblower program post-corruption scandal, strengthening its ethical governance.

5. **Leadership Training and Development**
    - Regularly train leaders on ethical decision-making, ESG principles, and the importance of integrity.
    - **Example:** Deloitte's ethics training programs equip leaders with tools to navigate ethical dilemmas.

6. **Transparent Reporting and Disclosure**
    - Adopt global standards for ESG reporting (e.g., GRI, SASB) to maintain accountability and build trust with stakeholders.
    - **Case Study:** Patagonia publishes detailed reports on its environmental and social initiatives, enhancing its reputation for ethical leadership.

Steps to Create an Ethical Governance Framework

1. **Assess Current Practices**

- Conduct a governance audit to identify gaps and areas of improvement in existing structures.
- **Example:** Apple's assessment of its supply chain governance led to enhanced labour rights policies.

2. **Engage Stakeholders**
   - Involve employees, customers, investors, and community representatives in designing governance policies.
   - **Case Study:** Starbucks engaged its partners and customers to co-create its ethical sourcing and sustainability policies.

3. **Define Ethical Leadership Competencies**
   - Establish behavioural indicators such as integrity, transparency, accountability, and inclusivity for leaders.
   - **Example:** Google's leadership framework emphasizes psychological safety and ethical decision-making.

4. **Implement Monitoring and Evaluation Mechanisms**
   - Regularly review governance processes to ensure their effectiveness and adapt to new challenges.
   - **Case Study:** Nestlé introduced independent third-party audits to verify its sustainability claims, maintaining its ethical commitment.

5. **Promote a Culture of Ethical Leadership**
   - Embed ethical principles into daily operations and recognize leaders who exemplify these values.
   - **Example:** Procter & Gamble's leadership incentives are tied to ethical performance metrics.

Impact of Ethical Governance Frameworks

1. **Enhanced Stakeholder Trust**
    - Transparent and ethical practices build confidence among investors, employees, and customers.
    - **Data Point:** Edelman's 2023 Trust Barometer found that 63% of people prefer to buy from companies they perceive as ethical.

2. **Risk Reduction**
    - Proactively addressing ethical risks prevents scandals, fines, and reputational damage.
    - **Case Study:** After implementing robust governance frameworks, Siemens reduced legal risks and regained investor confidence.

3. **Improved Financial Performance**
    - Ethical companies often outperform peers due to strong stakeholder relationships and sustainable practices.
    - **Example:** Companies on Ethisphere's *World's Most Ethical Companies* list consistently demonstrate above-average financial returns.

4. **Cultural Transformation**
    - Embedding governance frameworks fosters a culture of accountability and integrity across all levels of the organization.
    - **Case Study:** After recovering from an accounting scandal, Olympus rebuilt its governance to create a culture prioritizing transparency and ethics.

Conclusion

Ethical governance frameworks are critical for ensuring that leadership decisions reflect the highest standards of integrity. By embedding ethics into the organizational fabric and holding leaders accountable, companies can create sustainable value for all stakeholders. These frameworks not only prevent ethical breaches but also position organizations as trusted, responsible leaders in their industries.

Chapter 8: Tools and Processes for Balanced Decision-Making

The Olympic Business Model: Balancing qualitative and quantitative factors

Leveraging the Balanced Scorecard for strategic alignment

Using NPS and VOC analysis for continuous improvement

Tools and Processes for Balanced Decision-Making

Balanced decision-making ensures that organizational choices align with ethical standards, stakeholder needs, and long-term sustainability goals. By leveraging structured tools and processes, leaders can reduce biases, evaluate trade-offs, and achieve equitable outcomes. Below are essential tools and processes, supported by examples and case studies, for balanced decision-making.

1. Decision-Making Frameworks

1.1. Balanced Scorecard (BSC)

- **What It Does:** Aligns business activities with vision and strategy by balancing financial and non-financial metrics.
- **Key Components:** Financial, customer, internal processes, and learning & growth perspectives.
- **Example:** A manufacturing company used the BSC to prioritize investments in sustainable energy projects, balancing cost with environmental impact.
- **Outcome:** Improved energy efficiency by 25% and reduced operational costs by 15% over five years.

1.2. SWOT Analysis

- **What It Does:** Identifies internal strengths and weaknesses, and external opportunities and threats.
- **Use Case:** A retail chain used SWOT analysis to decide between opening new stores or enhancing e-commerce platforms.

- **Outcome:** Opted for e-commerce expansion, achieving 30% revenue growth in two years.

---

2. Analytical Tools

2.1. Decision Trees

- **What It Does:** Maps out possible outcomes of decisions and their implications.
- **Example:** A pharmaceutical firm used a decision tree to evaluate whether to invest in a high-risk R&D project.
- **Outcome:** Proceeded with the project based on high potential ROI; the resulting drug became a blockbuster, generating $2 billion in revenue.

2.2. Monte Carlo Simulations

- **What It Does:** Simulates different scenarios to assess risk and probability in complex decisions.
- **Case Study:** Airbus used Monte Carlo simulations to assess risks in its supply chain, minimizing disruptions.
- **Outcome:** Reduced supply chain costs by 20% and improved delivery timelines.

---

3. Collaborative Decision-Making Tools

3.1. Delphi Method

- **What It Does:** Collects expert opinions through multiple rounds to achieve a consensus.
- **Example:** The UN used the Delphi method to prioritize global sustainability initiatives.

- **Outcome:** Effective allocation of resources to high-impact areas like renewable energy and water conservation.

3.2. RACI Matrix

- **What It Does:** Clarifies roles and responsibilities (Responsible, Accountable, Consulted, Informed).
- **Example:** A tech startup used the RACI matrix to streamline decision-making in product development.
- **Outcome:** Reduced project delays by 40% and accelerated time-to-market.

4. Processes for Balanced Decision-Making

4.1. Stakeholder Engagement

- **Process:** Gather input from all stakeholders to ensure diverse perspectives.
- **Case Study:** Patagonia engaged employees, customers, and suppliers to design its sustainability strategy.
- **Outcome:** Enhanced brand loyalty and achieved a 10% annual revenue increase.

4.2. Root Cause Analysis (RCA)

- **Process:** Identify underlying causes of problems before making decisions.
- **Example:** Toyota's use of the "5 Whys" method to address production issues.
- **Outcome:** Reduced defects by 30% and improved customer satisfaction.

4.3. Scenario Planning

- **Process:** Evaluate multiple future scenarios to prepare for uncertainty.
- **Case Study:** Shell Oil uses scenario planning to anticipate energy market trends.
- **Outcome:** Maintained market leadership and adaptability through global shifts in energy policy.

---

5. Ethical Tools

5.1. Ethical Decision-Making Models

- **What It Does:** Ensures decisions align with moral principles like fairness, transparency, and accountability.
- **Example:** Johnson & Johnson's *Ethics Framework* guided its response to the Tylenol crisis.
- **Outcome:** Restored customer trust and preserved market share.

5.2. ESG Dashboards

- **What It Does:** Tracks environmental, social, and governance metrics to align decisions with sustainability goals.
- **Example:** Unilever's ESG dashboard helps prioritize sustainability initiatives.
- **Outcome:** Reduced carbon footprint by 50% and increased investor confidence.

---

6. AI-Driven Decision Tools

6.1. Predictive Analytics

- **What It Does:** Uses historical data to forecast outcomes.

- **Case Study:** Amazon employs predictive analytics to optimize inventory management.
- **Outcome:** Reduced inventory costs by 25% and improved delivery efficiency.

6.2. Natural Language Processing (NLP)

- **What It Does:** Analyses customer and employee feedback for insights.
- **Example:** A financial institution used NLP to identify patterns of dissatisfaction among customers.
- **Outcome:** Enhanced customer retention by 15%.

Impact of Balanced Decision-Making

1. **Improved Organizational Performance**
   - Data-driven decisions reduce errors and enhance efficiency.
   - **Statistic:** Companies using balanced scorecards report 34% higher profitability than peers.

2. **Enhanced Stakeholder Trust**
   - Transparent decision-making builds confidence among employees, investors, and customers.
   - **Example:** Starbucks' stakeholder-inclusive approach to decision-making resulted in consistent growth.

3. **Long-Term Sustainability**
   - Balanced decisions consider environmental and social impacts, ensuring future viability.
   - **Case Study:** Tesla's focus on renewable energy products aligns with long-term sustainability goals.

Conclusion

Implementing tools and processes for balanced decision-making enables organizations to navigate complexity, minimize risks, and achieve sustainable success. By combining analytical rigor with ethical considerations, leaders can create value for all stakeholders while securing their organization's future.

The Olympic Business Model: Balancing Qualitative and Quantitative factors

The **Olympic Business Model** integrates both qualitative and quantitative factors through an **Input-Process-Output (IPO)** framework to ensure alignment between organizational goals and operational execution. This dynamic model leverages structured circles of focus for both qualitative and quantitative aspects, driving performance in a **VUCA (Volatile, Uncertain, Complex, Ambiguous)** world.

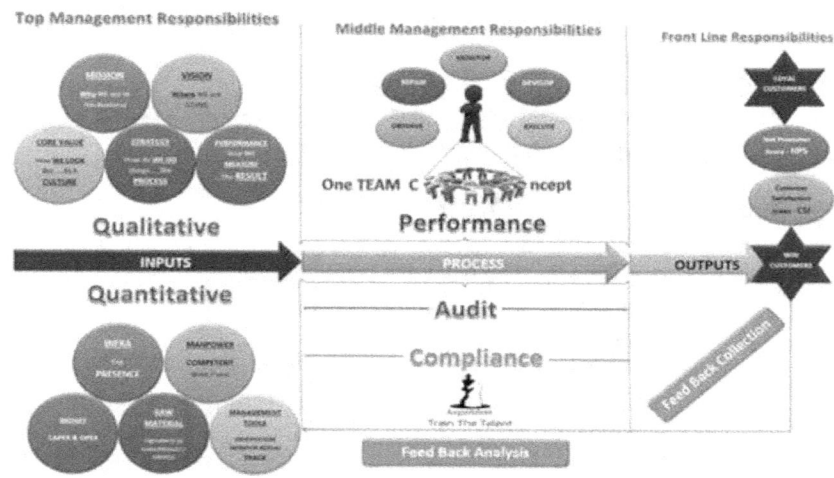

Olympic Business Model

Input: The Foundational Circles

5 Qualitative Circles

Corporate Examples for Each Area

---

1. Mission: Defining Purpose

Corporate Example: Patagonia

- **Mission:** "We're in business to save our home planet."
- **Purpose:** Patagonia's mission focuses on environmental sustainability, integrating its business model with conservation efforts.
- **How It Guides Activities:** The company emphasizes ethical sourcing, waste reduction, and funding environmental activism, making its mission central to all business decisions.
- **Impact:** Enhanced brand loyalty among eco-conscious consumers, driving both social impact and profitability.

---

2. Vision: Establishing Long-Term Goals

Corporate Example: Tesla

- **Vision:** "To create the most compelling car company of the 21st century by driving the world's transition to electric vehicles."
- **Aspirational Objective:** Tesla's vision directs its innovations in electric vehicles, batteries, and renewable energy solutions.
- **Implementation:** Heavy investments in R&D and scaling production to make EVs affordable and accessible globally.
- **Impact:** Tesla is now the market leader in electric vehicles, with a significant role in reducing carbon emissions.

3. Core Values: Shaping Organizational Behaviour

Corporate Example: Google

- **Core Values:** "Focus on the user and all else will follow" and "Do the right thing."
- **How It Shapes Culture:** Google's core values guide its innovation, emphasizing user-centric design, inclusivity, and ethical practices.
- **Example in Action:** Policies to ensure data privacy and user trust reflect its commitment to integrity.
- **Impact:** Google's strong culture fosters innovation, attracting top talent and maintaining customer trust.

---

4. Strategy: Defining Approaches

Corporate Example: Amazon

- **Strategy:** Customer obsession, operational excellence, and innovation.
- **Processes Designed:** Leveraging advanced logistics systems, AI-driven personalization, and scalable cloud infrastructure to meet customer needs.
- **Example in Action:** Amazon Prime's seamless delivery ecosystem highlights its strategic focus on customer convenience.
- **Impact:** Amazon's strategy has made it one of the most customer-centric and profitable companies globally.

---

5. People's Performance: Specifying Actions

Corporate Example: Toyota

- **Philosophy:** "Kaizen" (continuous improvement) and teamwork.

- **How People Perform:** Employees at all levels are encouraged to identify inefficiencies and contribute to process improvements.
- **Example in Action:** The Toyota Production System (TPS) empowers employees to stop the production line if issues arise, fostering accountability and quality.
- **Impact:** Toyota's emphasis on individual and team performance has made it a global leader in manufacturing efficiency and product quality.

Summary Table

Area	Corporate Example	Key Action/Impact
Mission	Patagonia	Focus on sustainability, driving brand loyalty and environmental activism.
Vision	Tesla	Accelerating global adoption of sustainable transportation and renewable energy.
Core Values	Google	Ethical and user-focused innovation fostering trust and talent attraction.
Strategy	Amazon	Customer-centric operational excellence driving market dominance.
People's Performance	Toyota	Empowered employees ensuring quality and efficiency through continuous improvement.

These examples demonstrate how clearly defined missions, visions, values, strategies, and people-centric processes can drive long-term success in diverse industries.

5 Quantitative Circles

1. Infrastructure

- **Corporate Example: Amazon**
    - **Application:** Combines extensive physical warehouses (fulfilment centres) with advanced digital platforms for inventory management and online shopping.
    - **Impact:** Enables Amazon to achieve rapid delivery speeds (e.g., Prime's two-day delivery) and handle high-order volumes efficiently.

2. Competent Manpower

- **Corporate Example: IBM**
    - **Application:** Implements a strategic workforce management plan by recruiting top talent and upskilling employees through its IBM SkillsBuild initiative.
    - **Impact:** Ensures a continuous supply of skilled personnel for AI, cloud, and quantum computing projects.

3. Fund Requirements

- **Corporate Example: Netflix**
    - **Application:** Invests heavily in content creation (CapEx) and global platform scaling (OpEx), funded through subscription revenue and strategic partnerships.
    - **Impact:** Netflix maintains its leadership in the streaming industry while generating sustainable revenue streams.

4. Technology and IT Systems

- **Corporate Example: Tesla**
    - **Application:** Leverages cutting-edge technology, such as AI-based autonomous driving systems, IoT sensors for vehicle monitoring, and efficient battery management tools.
    - **Impact:** Positions Tesla as a leader in innovation while delivering cost-effective and sustainable solutions.

5. Raw Materials

- **Corporate Example: Starbucks**
    - **Application:** Ensures ethical sourcing of coffee beans through its Coffee and Farmer Equity (C.A.F.E.) Practices program.
    - **Impact:** Maintains product quality while promoting sustainability and fair trade.

Corporate Examples for Quantitative Circles and Process Execution

Area	Corporate Example	Key Actions and Impact
Infrastructure	Amazon	Combines extensive physical warehouses with advanced digital platforms for inventory management and online shopping. Enables rapid delivery and scalability.
	Walmart	Integrates brick-and-mortar stores with e-commerce platforms, enabling curb side pickup and home delivery for enhanced customer convenience.
	Starbucks	Uses a hybrid model of physical stores and mobile ordering apps to optimize customer experience and reduce wait times.
Competent Manpower	IBM	Recruits and trains employees in emerging fields like AI and quantum computing through initiatives like IBM SkillsBuild.
	Google	Employs rigorous recruitment processes and continuous upskilling programs to maintain a workforce aligned with its innovation goals.
	Procter & Gamble (P&G)	Deploys cross-functional teams for product innovation, integrating insights from R&D, marketing, and operations.
Fund Requirements	Tesla	Balances CapEx for building Gigafactories and OpEx for R&D and operations, funded through equity, bonds, and pre-order revenues.
	Netflix	Invests heavily in original content production and platform development, supported by subscription-based revenues and strategic partnerships.
	Olympic Games	Uses sponsorships, broadcasting rights, and ticket sales to finance infrastructure and operational costs.
Technology and IT Systems	Apple	Leverages advanced supply chain management tools and proprietary software to enhance operational efficiency and product delivery timelines.
	Toyota	Implements IoT and AI technologies in manufacturing processes, ensuring high-quality production and waste reduction.
	Microsoft	Uses cloud-based tools and AI for real-time collaboration and data-driven decision-making.
	Starbucks	Sourcing through ethical practices under C.A.F.E. guidelines, ensuring product quality and sustainability.

Raw Materials	Nestlé	Adopts sustainable raw material sourcing practices for water, coffee, and other agricultural products.
	Coca-Cola	Focuses on water stewardship and sustainable packaging as key raw material initiatives.

Process: Operational Execution

1. One-Team Concept

- **Corporate Example: Procter & Gamble (P&G)**
    - o **Application:** Uses cross-functional teams for product development, combining insights from R&D, marketing, and supply chain management.
    - o **Impact:** Accelerates time-to-market for innovative products, like Tide Pods.

2. Monitoring & Development

- **Corporate Example: Toyota**
    - o **Application:** Uses the Toyota Production System (TPS) to monitor performance and implement continuous improvement (Kaizen).
    - o **Impact:** Reduces waste, improves quality, and enhances operational efficiency.

3. Audits and Compliance

- **Corporate Example: Unilever**
    - o **Application:** Conducts regular sustainability audits across its supply chain to ensure alignment with its Sustainable Living Plan.

- **Impact:** Builds stakeholder trust and ensures compliance with global sustainability standards.

Process Execution

Process Step	Corporate Example	Key Actions and Impact
One-Team Concept	Procter & Gamble (P&G)	Encourages collaboration among R&D, marketing, and operations teams for innovative product launches.
	Google	Cross-functional teams tackle complex projects like Google Cloud, enhancing innovation and efficiency.
Monitoring & Development	Toyota	Uses the Toyota Production System (TPS) to monitor processes and continuously improve efficiency and quality.
	Tesla	Monitors battery production and vehicle performance in real-time, addressing issues proactively.
Audits and Compliance	Unilever	Conducts regular sustainability audits to ensure compliance with its Sustainable Living Plan and global ESG standards.
	Siemens	Post-scandal compliance initiatives included frequent internal and external audits, restoring trust and improving governance.

Output: Results and Feedback

1. Result Evaluation

- **Corporate Example: Apple**
    - **Application:** Evaluates product success using metrics like Customer Satisfaction Index (CSI) and Net Promoter Score (NPS).
    - **Impact:** Consistently delivers high-performing products and maintains brand loyalty.

2. 360-Degree Feedback

- **Corporate Example: Accenture**
    - **Application:** Uses 360-degree feedback for leadership evaluation, incorporating perspectives from peers, subordinates, and clients.
    - **Impact:** Enhances leadership effectiveness and employee engagement.

3. Continuous Improvement

- **Corporate Example: GE (General Electric)**
    - **Application:** Incorporates Lean management principles to adapt processes in response to market dynamics.
    - **Impact:** Drives operational agility and long-term competitiveness.

Output and Feedback

Output Area	Corporate Example	Key Actions and Impact
Result Evaluation	Apple	Uses metrics like Customer Satisfaction Index (CSI) and NPS to assess product success and inform future improvements.
	Amazon	Regularly evaluates performance based on delivery timelines, customer feedback, and profitability metrics.
360-Degree Feedback	Accenture	Incorporates 360-degree reviews for leadership development, gathering input from peers, subordinates, and clients.
	Microsoft	Uses employee feedback surveys to align workplace practices with employee satisfaction and productivity.
Continuous Improvement	General Electric (GE)	Applies Lean management principles to adapt processes in response to dynamic market demands.
	IKEA	Implements circular economy practices, continuously updating operations to reduce waste and improve sustainability.

Benefits of the Olympic Business Model

1. Balanced Execution

- **Example:** Nike integrates innovation (e.g., Flyknit technology) with sustainability, achieving cost-effectiveness and high market appeal.

2. Stakeholder Trust

- **Example:** Microsoft's ESG transparency builds trust among customers, employees, and investors.

3. Sustainability

- **Example:** IKEA's circular economy initiatives reduce environmental impact while driving profitability.

This model demonstrates how companies can effectively integrate and balance quantitative resources and processes with qualitative goals to achieve sustainable, impactful results.

Leveraging the Balanced Scorecard for Strategic Alignment

The Balanced Scorecard (BSC) is a powerful tool for aligning strategy with performance across an organization, ensuring that initiatives are transparent, measurable, and linked to corporate goals. It provides a framework for both qualitative and quantitative assessments, helping leaders monitor progress in real-time and make informed decisions without resorting to manipulation or distortion of data.

Leveraging the Balanced Scorecard for Strategic Alignment

1. Comprehensive Strategic Alignment

- **What It Is:** The BSC connects an organization's strategy with specific performance metrics across four perspectives: Financial, Customer, Internal Processes, and Learning & Growth.

- **Application:** By integrating ESG goals with financial metrics, the BSC enables organizations to track both financial performance and sustainability initiatives.
- **Example:** Unilever uses the BSC to monitor sustainability goals, linking them with financial targets like revenue growth from sustainable products and cost savings from efficient resource use.

2. Real-Time Assessment of Performance

- **What It Does:** Provides real-time updates on key performance indicators (KPIs) linked to the strategy, allowing leaders to adjust strategies as needed.
- **Application:** Through dashboards and analytics, companies like Microsoft can quickly assess the impact of new technologies on customer satisfaction and operational efficiency.
- **Outcome:** This capability allows for quick responses to market changes, ensuring that strategic goals are met without manipulation of performance data.

3. Reducing Risk Through Transparency

- **What It Does:** By making strategic objectives and metrics visible, the BSC reduces the risk of data manipulation and ensures accountability.
- **Example:** IKEA uses the BSC to track emissions reductions, linking it directly with real-time operational data from its supply chain and logistics. This transparency ensures that any discrepancies are quickly identified and addressed.
- **Impact:** This approach builds trust with stakeholders by providing an honest and accurate reflection of performance.

4. Qualitative and Quantitative Insights

- **What It Does:** The BSC combines qualitative insights (e.g., customer satisfaction, employee engagement) with quantitative measures (e.g., revenue growth, cost reduction) to provide a balanced view of performance.

- **Application:** At Tesla, the BSC is used to balance production efficiency (quantitative) with innovative output and customer experience (qualitative), linking these to broader strategic objectives like global EV adoption.

- **Outcome:** This alignment ensures that every strategic initiative drives both short-term gains and long-term sustainability.

5. Continuous Feedback and Improvement

- **What It Does:** The BSC facilitates continuous feedback loops, integrating real-time data to adjust strategies and improve performance over time.

- **Example:** Google uses the BSC to monitor projects across its various initiatives, adapting to changing market demands and technological advancements.

- **Impact:** Regular updates and adjustments based on real-time data ensure that strategy remains relevant and effective.

Case Study: Apple

- **Application:** Apple uses the BSC to align product development with customer satisfaction metrics, incorporating insights from online feedback and sales data.

- **Outcome:** The BSC allows Apple to monitor performance across its diverse product lines, adjusting strategy in response to market changes and customer preferences without resorting to data manipulation.

Benefits of Using the BSC for Strategic Alignment

1. **Enhanced Decision-Making:** Leaders can make informed decisions by linking operational data directly with strategic goals, avoiding subjective biases.

2. **Improved Performance Management**: Regular monitoring allows for adjustments in real-time, ensuring that initiatives remain on track.

3. **Strengthened Governance**: By maintaining transparency, the BSC ensures that strategic decisions are made with integrity, enhancing stakeholder trust.

4. **Sustainability Focus**: Integrating ESG metrics into the BSC ensures that sustainability is embedded in the overall strategy, balancing long-term goals with immediate performance needs.

By using the Balanced Scorecard effectively, organizations can maintain strategic alignment, monitor performance accurately, and ensure that all decisions are made with integrity and transparency. This approach helps prevent manipulation, provides a clear view of business health, and supports sustainable, long-term growth.

Using NPS and VOC analysis for Continuous Improvement

Using Net Promoter Score (NPS) and Voice of the Customer (VOC) analysis for continuous improvement is a powerful way to gather real-time feedback from customers to enhance products, services, and overall customer experience. By focusing on these tools without resorting to manipulation, organizations can accurately measure satisfaction, identify areas for improvement, and drive growth in a sustainable manner.

NPS and VOC Analysis Without Manipulation

**1. Net Promoter Score (NPS)

- **What It Is**: NPS is a metric that measures customer loyalty by asking respondents to rate the likelihood of recommending a product or service on a scale from 0 to 10. Responses are categorized into promoters (9-10), passives (7-8), and detractors (0-6).

- **Use Case**: NPS is used by companies like Apple and Amazon to gauge customer satisfaction and loyalty.
- **Impact**: It provides a straightforward, quantitative measure of customer experience, allowing companies to track progress over time. By focusing on promoters (and increasing their number), companies can drive growth through word-of-mouth referrals.
- **Without Manipulation**: It's crucial to ensure that customer feedback remains honest and not influenced by incentives or selective feedback mechanisms. Using NPS purely for strategic insights, not for manipulation, allows companies to focus on real customer sentiment and implement effective changes

2. Voice of the Customer (VOC) Analysis

- **What It Is**: VOC involves capturing and interpreting customer feedback through surveys, reviews, social media, and other channels. It provides qualitative insights into customer needs, preferences, and issues.
- **Use Case**: Companies like Starbucks and Microsoft use VOC to understand customer needs and expectations across various touchpoints, from online interactions to physical stores.
- **Impact**: VOC enables companies to identify specific issues impacting customer experience, such as product quality, service delivery, or customer support. This feedback informs product development, customer service training, and marketing strategies.
- **Without Manipulation**: It's crucial to maintain the integrity of VOC data by using unbiased collection methods, like random sampling and unbiased question framing, to get a representative view of customer sentiment. This approach ensures that changes made based on VOC data are genuine improvements, not distortions of customer experience

Continuous Improvement Based on NPS and VOC

1. **Real-Time Data Utilization**: Companies can track changes in NPS and VOC scores frequently to monitor customer satisfaction and engagement. Real-time dashboards help leaders make quick, informed decisions.

2. **Actionable Insights**: By focusing on key themes in feedback (e.g., product reliability, customer support responsiveness), organizations can prioritize areas for improvement.

3. **Ongoing Monitoring and Adaptation**: Regularly reviewing NPS and VOC data ensures that any manipulative behaviours or misinterpretations of data are addressed promptly, leading to genuine customer-centric improvements.

By using NPS and VOC analysis without manipulation, organizations can gain an authentic understanding of customer experience, driving continuous improvement and building lasting customer relationships. This approach aligns with the principles of real-time performance assessment, ensuring that strategic decisions are based on accurate, unbiased customer feedback

Chapter 9: Re-Skilling and Future-Proofing Talent

Identifying skill gaps and creating development pathways

Building a culture of continuous learning and innovation

Examples of successful talent transformation programs

Re-Skilling and Future-Proofing Talent

Re-skilling and future-proofing talent are critical strategies for organizations to adapt to changing market demands and technological advancements. These initiatives ensure that employees have the necessary skills to remain competitive, innovate effectively, and contribute to long-term organizational success. Here's how organizations can approach re-skilling and future-proofing talent:

1. Importance of Re-Skilling

Re-skilling is essential in a rapidly evolving job market driven by automation, AI, and digital transformation. As industries shift, the ability to adapt and learn new skills quickly becomes crucial for job security and career progression. Organizations that invest in re-skilling not only protect their workforce from obsolescence but also enhance productivity and competitiveness.

- **Data and Impact**: A report by the World Economic Forum highlights that re-skilling initiatives can increase employee productivity by 5% to 15%. Companies investing in training programs see a return on investment through higher job satisfaction, reduced turnover, and improved adaptability

2. Key Strategies for Re-Skilling

- **Continuous Learning Programs**: Providing access to online courses, workshops, and certifications allows employees to keep pace with technological changes. Programs like Coursera and LinkedIn Learning offer a wide range of courses aligned with industry needs.

- **In-house Training Initiatives**: Organizations can establish in-house training academies to focus on specific skills required for the future. For instance, Google's in-house academy provides engineers with continuous education in AI and machine learning.
- **Partnerships with Educational Institutions**: Collaborating with universities and vocational schools to offer tailored curriculum and upskilling courses helps in addressing skill gaps early on.

3. Future-Proofing Talent

Futureproofing involves creating a flexible, adaptable workforce equipped to thrive in a VUCA (Volatile, Uncertain, Complex, Ambiguous) world. It's about embedding lifelong learning into corporate culture, preparing employees to navigate shifts in technology, business models, and market demands.

- **Scenario Planning and Simulation Exercises**: Organizations can use simulations to prepare employees for different future scenarios. For example, the military uses simulation to train personnel for complex operations; similarly, companies can simulate market disruptions to test strategic agility
- **Cross-Training and Job Rotation Programs**: These programs help employees gain exposure to different roles and departments, fostering a culture of learning and adaptability. Microsoft's 'Garage' initiative allows employees to work on innovative projects across departments, facilitating skill acquisition and cross-functional collaboration.

4. Using Data to Guide Re-Skilling Efforts

- **Skills Gap Analysis**: Regularly assess current employee skills versus required skills using tools like AI-driven analytics and machine learning algorithms. This helps identify where training is most needed.

- **Employee Feedback Systems**: Tools like NPS (Net Promoter Score) and 360-degree feedback mechanisms help gauge employee satisfaction and readiness for new skills.
- **Real-Time Assessment Platforms**: Use platforms like Degreed or Coursera to track employee learning and progress, linking this data to performance reviews and career development plans.

5. Role of Leadership in Re-Skilling Initiatives

- **Top Management Support**: Leaders must champion re-skilling by allocating budgets, setting expectations, and integrating re-skilling goals into performance reviews.
- **Promoting a Learning Culture**: Leaders should demonstrate continuous learning behaviors, like attending workshops and sharing insights from new courses, setting a precedent for the rest of the organization.

Impact of Re-Skilling and Future-Proofing

- **Enhanced Adaptability**: Organizations with strong re-skilling programs can quickly pivot in response to market changes, such as new regulatory requirements or emerging technologies.
- **Boosted Innovation**: A future-proofed workforce is more innovative, capable of driving digital transformation and breakthrough technologies.
- **Sustainability and Growth**: Continuous re-skilling supports sustainability by ensuring that employees are not only prepared for the future but also equipped to contribute to the organization's long-term success and sustainability goals.

By focusing on re-skilling and future-proofing talent, organizations can create a workforce that is resilient, adaptable, and ready to thrive in a dynamic business environment.

Identifying Skill Gaps and Creating Development Pathways

Identifying skill gaps and creating development pathways is essential for organizations to ensure their workforce remains competitive, agile, and aligned with strategic goals. This process involves evaluating current employee capabilities, recognizing where these skills do not meet organizational needs, and developing targeted training and development plans to bridge these gaps. Here's how organizations can effectively implement this process:

1. Identifying Skill Gaps

- **Skill Assessment Tools**: Regular use of skill gap analysis tools, such as AI-driven analytics, surveys, and competency assessments, helps to pinpoint where employees lack the necessary skills. These tools can measure proficiency in specific areas, such as data analytics, leadership, digital marketing, and technical expertise.

- **Example**: Microsoft uses AI-based skill gap analysis to evaluate technical skills across its workforce. The tool identifies underdeveloped skills related to cloud computing, machine learning, and cybersecurity, enabling targeted training programs.

- **Impact**: By identifying these gaps, organizations can tailor learning and development programs to address specific needs, increasing productivity and reducing time-to-market for new initiatives

2. Creating Development Pathways

- **Personalized Learning Plans**: Development pathways should be customized based on individual career aspirations, current roles, and skill requirements. These plans may include formal courses, online certifications, workshops, and hands-on projects.

- **Example**: At IBM, personalized learning plans are created using an integrated platform that combines in-house training courses with external educational partnerships. This approach ensures that employees have access to the latest knowledge and skills.

- **Impact**: This strategy not only prepares employees for their current roles but also positions them for future opportunities within the organization. It also contributes to higher employee engagement by allowing them to see a clear path for advancement

3. Building Effective Learning Paths

- **Blended Learning Approaches**: Combining classroom training, online courses, webinars, and hands-on experience allows for more flexible learning pathways. Blended learning can be particularly effective for technical skills that require practical application.
- **Example**: Google's Grow with Google initiative offers a combination of online courses, community workshops, and in-person boot camps to develop skills in high-demand areas like coding, digital marketing, and data analysis.
- **Impact**: This approach ensures comprehensive learning and adaptation, enabling employees to apply new skills directly to their work environment and ensuring they remain relevant in their roles

4. Role of Leadership in Skill Development

- **Leadership Commitment**: Senior management must actively support and invest in development programs, ensuring that re-skilling is aligned with the company's strategic priorities. Regular updates and communication from leadership can foster a learning culture within the organization.
- **Example**: Accenture's CEO has emphasized the importance of reskilling as part of the company's broader strategy, making it a key performance metric for managers and leaders. This ensures that skills development is integrated into everyday operations.
- **Impact**: When leaders prioritize development, it signals to the workforce that continuous learning is essential for career advancement and organizational success

5. Measuring Success

- **KPIs for Development Programs**: Organizations should use KPIs such as course completion rates, certification attainment, time-to-proficiency, and post-training performance metrics to evaluate the success of development pathways.

- **Example**: A company like SAP might track certification levels in cloud technologies, assessing how these new skills impact project delivery timelines and quality.

- **Impact**: Regular monitoring ensures that development pathways are effective, and adjustments can be made as needed, ensuring continuous improvement in skills and organizational performance

By systematically identifying skill gaps and creating tailored development pathways, organizations can not only enhance their workforce's capabilities but also drive innovation, agility, and long-term success in an increasingly complex and competitive environment.

Tables for Identifying Skill Gaps and Creating Development Pathways Based on the Competency Framework

Table 1: Identifying Skill Gaps and Creating Development Pathways for **Base-Level Employees**

Competency	Skill Gaps	Development Pathway
Communication	Limited ability to convey information clearly. Lack of active listening skills.	**Training Programs**: Enrol in courses on effective communication, public speaking, and active listening.
	Difficulty tailoring messages to different audiences.	**On-the-Job Experience**: Participate in role-playing scenarios to practice different communication styles.
Problem Solving	Weak analytical skills, slow to find solutions.	**Workshops**: Attend problem-solving workshops focused on logic, pattern recognition, and data analysis.
	Inability to think creatively under pressure.	**Mentoring**: Pair with mentors who can guide through complex problem-solving scenarios.
Teamwork	Struggles with collaboration and teamwork, often works in isolation.	**Team Projects**: Participate in group activities and projects to build cooperative skills.
	Poor adaptability to changes in team dynamics.	**Coaching Sessions**: Regular one-on-one sessions to discuss teamwork strategies and conflict resolution techniques.
Time Management	Inconsistent in managing workload and prioritizing tasks.	**Time Management Workshops**: Learn techniques for setting priorities, scheduling effectively, and reducing procrastination.
	Difficulty adapting to changes in project timelines.	**Training in Agile Methodologies**: Gain familiarity with agile project management principles to handle dynamic environments.
Adaptability	Slow to adopt new technologies or processes.	**Onboarding Sessions**: Learn new tools and technologies through training sessions and online tutorials.
	Resistance to changes in work procedures.	**Cross-Training**: Rotate through different roles or departments to gain experience in varied processes.
Customer Orientation	Inadequate understanding of customer needs and concerns.	**Customer Service Training**: Courses focusing on empathy, active listening, and handling customer complaints effectively.
	Inconsistent in providing solutions based on customer feedback.	**Feedback Loops**: Implement systems for continuous customer feedback and use it to tailor products and services.

Table 2: Identifying Skill Gaps and Creating Development Pathways for **Leadership/CXO Level Employees**

Competency	Skill Gaps	Development Pathway
Strategic Thinking	Lack of ability to anticipate market trends and long-term risks.	**Executive Coaching**: Work with a coach on scenario planning and strategic foresight exercises.
	Difficulty integrating data from various functions into strategic decisions.	**Leadership Seminars**: Attend workshops on integrated strategy development and cross-functional collaboration.
Executive Leadership	Inability to inspire and lead diverse teams.	**Leadership Training**: Participate in leadership programs focused on emotional intelligence and team dynamics.
	Weak in crisis management and handling complex challenges.	**Crisis Simulation Exercises**: Regularly participate in simulations to develop crisis response strategies.
Financial Acumen	Inadequate knowledge of complex financial models and market analysis.	**Advanced Financial Workshops**: Attend courses on financial modelling, risk assessment, and strategic investment planning.
	Difficulty managing budgets across multiple departments.	**Executive Budgeting Training**: Gain skills in allocation of resources and understanding departmental needs.
Decision Making	Slow to make decisions under uncertainty or with incomplete information.	**Decision-Making Simulations**: Practice real-time decision-making scenarios to build confidence and speed.
	Inconsistent use of data-driven insights for strategic choices.	**Data Analysis Courses**: Enrol in courses on data analytics, interpretation, and application in business strategy.
Change Management	Resistance to implementing organizational changes effectively.	**Change Leadership Workshops**: Gain skills in managing change, communication strategies, and stakeholder engagement.
	Inability to align team and organizational goals during transitions.	**Team Alignment Exercises**: Conduct regular workshops and retreats to align leadership and team objectives.
Cultural Awareness	Limited understanding of global markets and diverse cultures.	**Cultural Competency Training**: Participate in programs that focus on cross-cultural communication and global market dynamics.

| | Poor engagement with external stakeholders (investors, media, and regulators). | **Stakeholder Engagement Workshops**: Learn techniques for effective communication and negotiation with diverse groups. |

Building a culture of continuous Learning and Innovation

Creating a culture of continuous learning and innovation involves fostering an environment where employees are encouraged to develop new skills, explore creative solutions, and embrace change. This culture ensures that the organization stays competitive, agile, and capable of addressing evolving market demands. Below are the core principles, strategies, and best practices for building such a culture:

1. Establish a Learning-Centric Vision

- **Define Organizational Values:** Align the company's mission and vision with continuous learning and innovation as core values.
- **Leadership Commitment:** Leaders should model learning behaviour, emphasizing its importance through their actions. For example, Satya Nadella's emphasis on a "growth mindset" transformed Microsoft's culture, spurring innovation and collaboration.

2. Encourage Lifelong Learning

- **Structured Training Programs:** Offer access to online courses, certifications, and in-house training.
    - **Example:** AT&T launched its "Workforce 2020" initiative to upskill employees in digital and technical fields, resulting in increased retention and adaptability.

- **On-the-Job Learning:** Facilitate opportunities like job rotation, cross-functional projects, and stretch assignments to reinforce hands-on learning.

3. Foster Collaboration and Knowledge Sharing

- **Cross-Functional Teams:** Encourage diverse teams to work together, leveraging different perspectives for innovative solutions.
    - **Example:** Procter & Gamble's Connect+Develop model uses external collaborations to drive product innovation.
- **Internal Knowledge Platforms:** Create forums or platforms where employees can share insights and lessons learned, like Google's internal tools for innovation sharing.

4. Create a Safe Space for Experimentation

- **Promote a Growth Mindset:** Encourage employees to take calculated risks without fear of failure, viewing mistakes as opportunities to learn.
    - **Example:** Amazon's "Day 1" philosophy fosters an environment where employees are empowered to experiment, leading to innovations like AWS.
- **Provide Resources:** Allocate budgets and time for innovation projects, hackathons, and brainstorming sessions.

5. Integrate Continuous Feedback Mechanisms

- **360-Degree Feedback:** Use comprehensive feedback systems to identify learning gaps and opportunities.
- **Customer-Centric Feedback:** Incorporate insights from Voice of the Customer (VOC) programs to align innovation with market needs.

6. Leverage Technology for Learning and Innovation

- **AI-Driven Platforms:** Use AI tools to personalize learning paths and identify emerging trends.
    - **Example:** IBM uses AI to recommend training programs based on employees' skill gaps and career aspirations.
- **Innovation Labs:** Establish spaces equipped with cutting-edge tools where employees can develop and test new ideas.

7. Recognize and Reward Learning and Innovation

- **Incentive Programs:** Offer rewards and recognition for employees who successfully implement new ideas or complete skill enhancement programs.
    - **Example:** 3M's 15% rule allows employees to dedicate a portion of their time to pursue innovative projects, which has resulted in groundbreaking products like Post-it Notes.

8. Measure and Refine the Learning and Innovation Process

- **Key Performance Indicators (KPIs):** Track metrics such as training completion rates, innovation ROI, and employee engagement in development programs.
- **Continuous Improvement:** Use data from performance assessments and feedback mechanisms to refine the learning and innovation ecosystem.

Outcomes of Building a Continuous Learning and Innovation Culture

1. **Increased Agility:** Employees are better equipped to adapt to technological and market changes.

2. **Enhanced Productivity:** Continuous learning improves skill proficiency and operational efficiency.

3. **Stronger Employee Retention:** A culture that values development fosters loyalty and reduces turnover.

4. **Sustainable Innovation:** By encouraging experimentation and collaboration, organizations consistently develop innovative solutions.

By prioritizing continuous learning and innovation, organizations not only future-proof their workforce but also maintain a competitive edge in dynamic markets. This cultural shift requires commitment at all levels, but its long-term benefits—enhanced agility, innovation, and resilience—are invaluable.

365-Day Learning Calendar Based on Skill Gaps

Table 1: Base-Level Employees

Month	Skill Focus	Activities	Tools & Methods	Expected Outcome
Jan	Communication Skills	Workshops on effective communication and active listening.	Role-playing exercises, real-time feedback tools.	Improved clarity and teamwork communication.
Feb	Time Management	Training sessions on prioritization and scheduling.	Time-blocking tools, Agile training for dynamic adaptability.	Enhanced task prioritization and productivity.
Mar	Team Collaboration	Group activities focusing on conflict resolution and cooperation.	Collaboration software like Slack, Trello, or Miro.	Better inter-team relationships and reduced conflicts.

Apr	Problem-Solving Skills	Analytical thinking workshops.	Problem-solving frameworks, case studies, simulations.	Faster and more effective resolution of work challenges.
May	Customer Orientation	Sessions on empathy and customer service excellence.	NPS feedback analysis, customer role-play simulations.	Increased customer satisfaction and retention rates.
Jun	Adaptability to Technology	Introductory training on company tools and systems.	Onboarding new tools like CRM platforms or collaborative IT tools.	Improved adoption of workplace technology.
Jul	Data Literacy	Foundational courses on basic analytics.	Excel, Tableau introduction, real-world data exercises.	Basic data interpretation and reporting skills.
Aug	Safety Compliance	Safety protocols and compliance workshops.	LMS compliance modules, on-site drills.	Increased adherence to safety standards.
Sep	Process Optimization	Lean process workshops.	Lean Six Sigma fundamentals, process mapping tools.	Enhanced operational efficiency.
Oct	Feedback Utilization	Sessions on interpreting and acting on feedback.	Anonymous survey analysis, team debriefs.	Improved personal growth and team alignment.
Nov	Cultural Awareness	Diversity and inclusion workshops.	Scenario-based learning, external speakers.	Greater workplace inclusivity and cross-cultural skills.
Dec	Year-End Skill Review	Performance review and calibration.	Peer assessments, team presentations.	Highlighting growth areas and next-year targets.

Table 2: Leadership/CXO-Level Employees

Month	Skill Focus	Activities	Tools & Methods	Expected Outcome
Jan	Strategic Thinking	Scenario planning and trend analysis.	Strategy simulation tools, Harvard Business Review cases.	Enhanced foresight and decision-making skills.
Feb	Change Management	Workshops on leading organizational transformation.	Interactive simulations, role-play.	Improved ability to manage resistance and transitions.
Mar	Advanced Data Analytics	Training on leveraging analytics for decision-making.	Tableau, Power BI, real-time organizational dashboards.	Data-driven strategic insights.
Apr	Stakeholder Engagement	Building and managing stakeholder relationships.	Stakeholder mapping tools, role-playing scenarios.	Strengthened investor and stakeholder trust.
May	Executive Leadership	Leadership retreats focusing on vision alignment.	Vision-crafting frameworks, group think-tank sessions.	Clear and aligned organizational vision.
Jun	ESG Integration	Training on aligning ESG with corporate goals.	ESG frameworks (GRI, SASB), sustainability dashboards.	Better ESG compliance and reporting.
Jul	Crisis Management	Crisis response simulations.	Crisis management workshops, situational role-play.	Enhanced resilience and response effectiveness.
Aug	Innovation Leadership	Hackathons and innovation labs.	Design thinking workshops, external collaboration tools.	Increased innovation pipeline and ideation capacity.
Sep	Ethical Decision-Making	Case studies on corporate ethics.	Ethical frameworks, interactive debate sessions.	Stronger integrity in leadership decisions.
Oct	Financial Acumen	Advanced financial strategy workshops.	Financial modeling, ROI analysis tools.	Better management of financial resources.

Nov	Cultural Intelligence	Cross-cultural leadership training.	Global business case studies, multicultural role-playing.	Improved cross-cultural collaboration.
Dec	Year-End Strategy Review	Strategy review and recalibration.	KPI dashboards, executive feedback sessions.	Refined strategies aligned with organizational goals.

2. Unbiased Learning Scorecard for Calibration

Category	Metric	Base-Level Employees	Leadership/CXO Level Employees
Knowledge Acquisition	% Completion of Assigned Learning Programs	≥85%	≥90%
Skill Application	Peer/Manager Assessment of Applied Skills	4/5 Rating	4.5/5 Rating
Innovation Impact	Number of Ideas Implemented	≥2 Per Quarter	≥5 Per Quarter
Team Collaboration	360-Degree Feedback Scores	≥80% Positive	≥90% Positive
Customer Orientation	Improvement in NPS Score	+10% Over Baseline	+15% Over Baseline
Growth Potential	GE-McKinsey 9-Box Placement	>60% in High-Performing Boxes	>80% in High-Performing Boxes

Calibration Using the GE-McKinsey 9-Box Framework

Building AugusTalent

Augustalent

Potential Assessment	Performance Assessment – Low	Performance Assessment – Moderate	Performance Assessment – High
High	"Rough Diamond" — Low Performer/High Potential	"Future Star" — Moderate Performer/High Potential	"Consistent Star" — High Performer/High Potential
Moderate	"Inconsistent Player" — Low Performer/Moderate Potential	"Key Player" — Moderate Performer/Moderate Potential	"Current Star" — High Performer/Moderate Potential
Low	"Talent Risk" — Low Performer/Low Potential	"Solid Professional" — Moderate Performer/Low Potential	"High Professional" — High Performer/Low Potential

AUGUSTALENTs are High Potential & High Performing Professional – having very "**High Learning Agility**", can **adapt** & **adopt PROCESSES** quickly and **PERFORM** to achieve the Business Targets (**RESULTS**)

1. **High Performers**: Individuals with top scores in knowledge, application, and impact are placed in high-performing boxes.
2. **Potential Movers**: Employees showing improvement in learning and application are tracked for next-tier opportunities.
3. **Development Needs**: Tailored development plans for employees needing additional training or coaching to move into high-performing categories.

This dual-table and learning scorecard framework ensures structured learning pathways while maintaining transparency and accountability for individual and organizational growth.

Examples of successful Talent Transformation Programs

Organizations across industries have implemented impactful talent transformation programs to adapt to changing business environments, technological advancements, and workforce expectations. Below are notable examples of successful initiatives that have driven measurable outcomes:

1. AT&T - Workforce 2020

- **Objective**: Transform the workforce to meet the demands of emerging technologies like 5G, AI, and cloud computing.
- **Key Initiatives**:
    - Invested over $1 billion in employee re-skilling programs.
    - Offered employees access to online training platforms (Udacity and Coursera) to acquire new technical skills.
    - Created career paths aligned with future business needs and encouraged self-directed learning.
- **Outcome**:
    - Over 50% of AT&T's workforce underwent skill transformation, significantly reducing the need for external hiring.
    - Enhanced employee retention and positioned AT&T as a leader in the telecommunications sector.

2. Unilever - Future-Fit Plan

- **Objective**: Build a purpose-driven workforce equipped to navigate sustainability and digital transformation challenges.
- **Key Initiatives**:

- Introduced personalized learning platforms for employees, focusing on sustainability, digital marketing, and data analytics.
- Partnered with organizations like LinkedIn Learning and Degreed for continuous development.
- Integrated a career transition program to help employees move into emerging roles within or outside the company.

- **Outcome**:
  - Increased internal mobility by 20%, ensuring alignment between employee aspirations and business needs.
  - Strengthened Unilever's position as a sustainable and innovative company.

3. Amazon - Upskilling 2025

- **Objective**: Equip employees with future-ready skills to meet the demands of automation and AI.
- **Key Initiatives**:
  - Committed $700 million to train 100,000 employees in areas like machine learning, robotics, and cloud computing.
  - Launched programs like the **AWS Academy**, which provides training in cloud computing, and the **Mechatronics and Robotics Apprenticeship** program.
  - Focused on helping employees transition into high-demand technical roles within Amazon or elsewhere.
- **Outcome**:
  - Employees gained certifications and technical skills, reducing Amazon's dependency on external recruitment for specialized roles.

- Improved employee satisfaction and talent retention.

4. Infosys - Digital Talent Transformation

- **Objective**: Transition the workforce from legacy IT roles to digital technologies like AI, machine learning, and blockchain.
- **Key Initiatives**:
    - Implemented a comprehensive training platform, **Lex**, offering on-demand digital learning modules.
    - Established partnerships with global universities to offer certifications in advanced technologies.
    - Focused on experiential learning through hackathons and real-world problem-solving.
- **Outcome**:
    - Re-skilled 200,000 employees, enabling Infosys to secure high-value digital transformation projects.
    - Enhanced client satisfaction due to increased agility and technical expertise within teams.

5. Google - Project Oxygen

- **Objective**: Enhance leadership capabilities and build a culture of continuous learning and innovation.
- **Key Initiatives**:
    - Identified key traits of successful managers through extensive research.
    - Designed leadership development programs focusing on communication, coaching, and employee engagement.

- ○ Launched ongoing feedback loops and mentoring initiatives to support leaders.

- **Outcome**:
  - ○ Improved team performance metrics, with manager effectiveness scores increasing by 75%.
  - ○ Strengthened employee satisfaction and retention, contributing to Google's reputation as a top employer.

6. Tata Steel - DigiTALeap

- **Objective**: Upskill the workforce in digital tools and analytics to drive innovation in manufacturing and operations.

- **Key Initiatives**:
  - ○ Conducted workshops on digital twin technology, predictive analytics, and IoT.
  - ○ Established "Digital Champions" programs to recognize employees leading digital initiatives.
  - ○ Collaborated with academic institutions to create specialized courses.

- **Outcome**:
  - ○ Significant improvements in operational efficiency and cost reduction.
  - ○ Cultivated a workforce ready to embrace Industry 4.0 innovations.

Key Takeaways from Successful Programs

1. **Alignment with Organizational Goals**: Programs must directly address the company's strategic priorities and future business needs.

2. **Personalized Learning Paths**: Tailoring development opportunities to individual needs ensures higher engagement and impact.

3. **Partnerships for Expertise**: Collaborations with educational platforms and industry leaders enhance the quality of training.

4. **Ongoing Support**: Continuous learning platforms, mentorship, and feedback loops ensure lasting skill development.

5. **Measurement and Outcomes**: Regularly assess the impact of programs using metrics like employee retention, internal mobility, and business performance.

These examples illustrate how strategic talent transformation initiatives can position organizations for long-term success while empowering employees to thrive in dynamic environments.

Chapter 10: Building a Legacy of Ethical Management

Developing a culture admired for integrity and maturity

Ensuring profitability and sustainability through ethical governance

Inspiring future leaders to redefine management without manipulation

Building a Legacy of Ethical Management

Organizations across industries have implemented impactful talent transformation programs to adapt to changing business environments, technological advancements, and workforce expectations. Below are notable examples of successful initiatives that have driven measurable outcomes:

1. AT&T - Workforce 2020

- **Objective**: Transform the workforce to meet the demands of emerging technologies like 5G, AI, and cloud computing.
- **Key Initiatives**:
    - Invested over $1 billion in employee re-skilling programs.
    - Offered employees access to online training platforms (Udacity and Coursera) to acquire new technical skills.
    - Created career paths aligned with future business needs and encouraged self-directed learning.
- **Outcome**:
    - Over 50% of AT&T's workforce underwent skill transformation, significantly reducing the need for external hiring.
    - Enhanced employee retention and positioned AT&T as a leader in the telecommunications sector.

2. Unilever - Future-Fit Plan

- **Objective**: Build a purpose-driven workforce equipped to navigate sustainability and digital transformation challenges.

- **Key Initiatives**:
    - Introduced personalized learning platforms for employees, focusing on sustainability, digital marketing, and data analytics.
    - Partnered with organizations like LinkedIn Learning and Degreed for continuous development.
    - Integrated a career transition program to help employees move into emerging roles within or outside the company.

- **Outcome**:
    - Increased internal mobility by 20%, ensuring alignment between employee aspirations and business needs.
    - Strengthened Unilever's position as a sustainable and innovative company.

---

3. Amazon - Upskilling 2025

- **Objective**: Equip employees with future-ready skills to meet the demands of automation and AI.

- **Key Initiatives**:
    - Committed $700 million to train 100,000 employees in areas like machine learning, robotics, and cloud computing.
    - Launched programs like the **AWS Academy**, which provides training in cloud computing, and the **Mechatronics and Robotics Apprenticeship** program.

- - Focused on helping employees transition into high-demand technical roles within Amazon or elsewhere.
- **Outcome**:
  - Employees gained certifications and technical skills, reducing Amazon's dependency on external recruitment for specialized roles.
  - Improved employee satisfaction and talent retention.

4. Infosys - Digital Talent Transformation

- **Objective**: Transition the workforce from legacy IT roles to digital technologies like AI, machine learning, and blockchain.
- **Key Initiatives**:
  - Implemented a comprehensive training platform, **Lex**, offering on-demand digital learning modules.
  - Established partnerships with global universities to offer certifications in advanced technologies.
  - Focused on experiential learning through hackathons and real-world problem-solving.
- **Outcome**:
  - Re-skilled 200,000 employees, enabling Infosys to secure high-value digital transformation projects.
  - Enhanced client satisfaction due to increased agility and technical expertise within teams.

5. Google - Project Oxygen

- **Objective**: Enhance leadership capabilities and build a culture of continuous learning and innovation.

- **Key Initiatives**:
  - Identified key traits of successful managers through extensive research.
  - Designed leadership development programs focusing on communication, coaching, and employee engagement.
  - Launched ongoing feedback loops and mentoring initiatives to support leaders.
- **Outcome**:
  - Improved team performance metrics, with manager effectiveness scores increasing by 75%.
  - Strengthened employee satisfaction and retention, contributing to Google's reputation as a top employer.

6. Tata Steel - DigiTALeap

- **Objective**: Upskill the workforce in digital tools and analytics to drive innovation in manufacturing and operations.
- **Key Initiatives**:
  - Conducted workshops on digital twin technology, predictive analytics, and IoT.
  - Established "Digital Champions" programs to recognize employees leading digital initiatives.
  - Collaborated with academic institutions to create specialized courses.
- **Outcome**:
  - Significant improvements in operational efficiency and cost reduction.

o Cultivated a workforce ready to embrace Industry 4.0 innovations.

Key Takeaways from Successful Programs

1. **Alignment with Organizational Goals**: Programs must directly address the company's strategic priorities and future business needs.

2. **Personalized Learning Paths**: Tailoring development opportunities to individual needs ensures higher engagement and impact.

3. **Partnerships for Expertise**: Collaborations with educational platforms and industry leaders enhance the quality of training.

4. **Ongoing Support**: Continuous learning platforms, mentorship, and feedback loops ensure lasting skill development.

5. **Measurement and Outcomes**: Regularly assess the impact of programs using metrics like employee retention, internal mobility, and business performance.

These examples illustrate how strategic talent transformation initiatives can position organizations for long-term success while empowering employees to thrive in dynamic environments.

Developing a culture admired for Integrity and Maturity

A culture of integrity and maturity is fundamental to building trust, fostering innovation, and ensuring long-term organizational success. Such a culture reflects honesty, ethical decision-making, transparency, and accountability at every level, combined with the emotional intelligence and resilience to navigate challenges effectively.

Key Strategies to Build a Culture of Integrity and Maturity

1. Set the Tone at the Top

- **Why It Matters:** Leadership plays a critical role in modeling ethical behaviour and setting organizational expectations.
- **How to Implement:**
    - Establish a **Code of Ethics** that defines acceptable behavior and decision-making standards.
    - Regularly communicate the importance of integrity and maturity through internal memos, town halls, and one-on-one interactions.
    - **Example:** Johnson & Johnson's *Credo* emphasizes its commitment to customers, employees, and society, creating a benchmark for integrity.

---

2. Foster Transparent Communication

- **Why It Matters:** Transparency reduces misunderstandings and builds trust between management and employees.
- **How to Implement:**
    - Regularly share updates on company performance, challenges, and changes through clear communication channels.
    - Encourage open dialogue where employees feel safe to voice concerns without fear of retaliation.
    - **Example:** Salesforce's **Ohana Culture** fosters transparency and employee feedback, contributing to a high-trust environment.

3. Build Accountability Systems

- **Why It Matters:** Accountability ensures that integrity is upheld across all levels.

- **How to Implement:**
    - Implement performance management systems tied to ethical behaviour.
    - Use **regular audits** to identify and address unethical practices.
    - Establish whistleblower policies to empower employees to report misconduct safely.
    - **Example:** Siemens strengthened its compliance systems and accountability mechanisms post-scandal, restoring stakeholder trust.

4. Emphasize Emotional Maturity

- **Why It Matters:** Emotional intelligence (EQ) allows employees to navigate complex relationships and situations with empathy and resilience.

- **How to Implement:**
    - Provide training on conflict resolution, active listening, and emotional intelligence.
    - Include EQ as a key component in leadership assessments.
    - **Example:** Google's *Project Aristotle* highlighted the importance of psychological safety and emotional intelligence for effective teams.

5. Recognize and Reward Ethical Behaviour

- **Why It Matters:** Reinforcing positive behaviour encourages others to follow suit.

- **How to Implement:**
    - Celebrate employees who exemplify integrity through recognition programs and public acknowledgment.
    - Tie incentives to ethical behaviour, not just performance metrics.
    - **Example:** Patagonia recognizes employees who lead sustainability and ethical initiatives, reinforcing its values.

---

6. Integrate Maturity into Decision-Making

- **Why It Matters:** Mature organizations can balance short-term gains with long-term sustainability and fairness.

- **How to Implement:**
    - Encourage decision-making frameworks that weigh the impact on all stakeholders, including employees, customers, and society.
    - Provide training on systems thinking and long-term planning.
    - **Example:** Unilever's *Sustainable Living Plan* integrates ESG goals into strategic decisions, demonstrating maturity in balancing profits with purpose.

---

7. Continuous Learning and Feedback

- **Why It Matters:** Organizations must adapt and evolve to maintain integrity and maturity in a dynamic environment.

- **How to Implement:**
    - Use 360-degree feedback to gather insights from employees, customers, and partners.
    - Provide continuous learning opportunities on ethics, leadership, and resilience.
    - **Example:** Accenture integrates learning programs for leadership to stay aligned with ethical and global sustainability standards.

Measuring Success

- **Employee Engagement Surveys**: Assess trust in leadership and perceptions of organizational integrity.
- **Customer Feedback (NPS and VOC)**: Evaluate trust and satisfaction levels to ensure alignment with ethical practices.
- **Compliance and Audit Reports**: Monitor adherence to ethical policies and identify areas for improvement.
- **Whistleblower Activity**: Use reported cases as an indicator of ethical awareness and accountability.

Benefits of a Culture of Integrity and Maturity

1. **Stronger Stakeholder Trust**: Builds credibility with employees, customers, and investors.
2. **Enhanced Employee Retention**: A fair and transparent culture reduces turnover.
3. **Sustainable Growth**: Ethical decision-making aligns with long-term success.

4. **Resilience in Crises**: Mature organizations are better equipped to navigate challenges with clarity and composure.

By embedding these principles, organizations can create an admired culture that fosters integrity, maturity, and lasting success.

Developing a Culture Admired for Integrity and Maturity with a Focus on Organizational Maturity Index

An **Organizational Maturity Index (OMI)** evaluates how well a company aligns its culture, processes, and systems with its strategic goals, ethical values, and operational excellence. Integrating integrity and maturity into the culture enhances trust, accountability, and the ability to navigate complex challenges. Below is a roadmap to achieve this, focusing on both qualitative cultural shifts and measurable improvements in OMI.

1. The Role of the Organizational Maturity Index

The **OMI** provides a structured framework to evaluate an organization's ability to:

- Embed integrity and maturity in leadership and decision-making.
- Maintain operational efficiency and resilience.
- Adapt to internal and external changes effectively.
- Align processes with strategic objectives.

Key Components of OMI:

1. **Governance and Leadership**: How well ethical leadership drives decision-making and compliance.
2. **Process Optimization**: The efficiency and transparency of workflows and accountability mechanisms.
3. **Cultural Alignment**: The integration of core values like integrity and inclusivity.

4. **Performance Metrics**: Real-time assessments of KPIs linked to ethical and operational objectives.

5. **Adaptability**: Agility in responding to changes in the business environment.

---

2. Strategies for Building Integrity and Maturity

a. Governance and Ethical Leadership

- **Action**: Establish a leadership framework that prioritizes ethical decision-making and long-term impact.
- **Example**: Johnson & Johnson's *Credo* reinforces ethical governance, guiding leadership during crises like the Tylenol recall.
- **OMI Impact**: Improves the **Governance** and **Leadership Maturity Score** by embedding ethics into core decision-making processes.

b. Transparent and Inclusive Culture

- **Action**: Develop channels for open communication, ensuring employees feel valued and heard.
- **Example**: Unilever regularly engages employees and stakeholders to align on sustainability and ethical goals.
- **OMI Impact**: Enhances **Cultural Alignment Metrics**, promoting trust and reducing turnover.

c. Comprehensive Learning and Development

- **Action**: Design training programs focusing on emotional intelligence (EQ), ethical decision-making, and stakeholder engagement.
- **Example**: Google's *Project Oxygen* improved leadership effectiveness by training managers on emotional maturity and communication.

- **OMI Impact**: Boosts **Process Maturity** by integrating advanced decision-making frameworks.

d. Accountability and Compliance Systems

- **Action**: Implement audits and performance reviews tied to ethical behavior.
- **Example**: Siemens rebuilt its governance mechanisms post-scandal, incorporating regular compliance audits.
- **OMI Impact**: Increases **Accountability Index** by ensuring alignment with ethical standards.

e. Continuous Feedback and Improvement

- **Action**: Use tools like NPS and VOC to gather employee and customer feedback for alignment with integrity goals.
- **Example**: Salesforce uses feedback loops to improve decision-making processes.
- **OMI Impact**: Strengthens the **Adaptability and Feedback Maturity Score**, enabling continuous improvement.

3. Measuring Organizational Maturity

OMI Dimension	Description	Measurement Metric
Governance and Ethics	Strength of leadership's commitment to integrity and ethical governance.	Whistleblower reports, compliance audit results, leadership EQ.
Cultural Alignment	Extent to which core values are embedded in employee behavior and decision-making.	Employee engagement scores, diversity metrics, value alignment.
Operational Processes	Efficiency, transparency, and adaptability of workflows.	Process efficiency ratios, time-to-resolution for escalations.
Stakeholder Trust	Level of trust among employees, customers, investors, and communities.	NPS, VOC scores, investor confidence ratings.

| Resilience and Agility | Ability to adapt to VUCA (Volatile, Uncertain, Complex, Ambiguous) environments. | Crisis response time, scenario planning effectiveness. |

4. Case Studies of Organizational Maturity and Cultural Integrity

a. Tata Group

- **Initiative**: Tata has a long-standing reputation for ethical leadership and stakeholder trust, driven by its governance framework.
- **Outcome**: High levels of employee loyalty and customer satisfaction, reflected in a strong Organizational Maturity Index.

b. Patagonia

- **Initiative**: Focused on transparency, sustainability, and stakeholder engagement.
- **Outcome**: Achieved both cultural and operational excellence, driving business growth and resilience.

c. Toyota

- **Initiative**: Uses the Toyota Production System (TPS) to embed quality and accountability at all levels.
- **Outcome**: Improved **Process Maturity** and trust through consistent product reliability.

5. Building a High-OMI Culture

- **Step 1**: Conduct baseline OMI assessments to identify gaps in governance, culture, and processes.
- **Step 2**: Develop targeted interventions, such as leadership training, process optimizations, and enhanced communication channels.
- **Step 3**: Monitor progress using OMI metrics, real-time feedback, and KPIs.

- **Step 4**: Align all improvements with core organizational values and long-term objectives.

Benefits of High Organizational Maturity

1. **Enhanced Trust**: Builds credibility with stakeholders, including employees, customers, and investors.
2. **Resilience in Crises**: Mature organizations handle disruptions more effectively.
3. **Sustainable Growth**: Ethical and transparent practices lead to long-term profitability.
4. **Employee Retention**: A culture rooted in integrity attracts and retains top talent.

By focusing on integrity and aligning with the Organizational Maturity Index, companies can build a culture that not only achieves operational success but also earns admiration and trust across all stakeholders.

Ensuring profitability and sustainability through Ethical Governance

Ethical governance is essential for balancing profitability and sustainability in today's business environment. Organizations that adhere to transparent, accountable, and ethical practices build trust with stakeholders, ensure regulatory compliance, and drive long-term success. Here's how ethical governance can simultaneously achieve these goals:

1. Governance as the Foundation for Profitability and Sustainability

Ethical governance creates a framework where decisions align with financial goals and environmental, social, and governance (ESG) principles. This framework ensures that short-term profits do not compromise long-term viability.

- **Example**: **Unilever** embeds sustainability into its governance, using its *Sustainable Living Plan* to link financial growth with environmental and social benefits. The company achieved €1 billion in annual sales from sustainable brands while reducing its carbon footprint.

2. Key Pillars of Ethical Governance

a. Transparency and Accountability

- **Why It Matters**: Transparent reporting builds stakeholder trust and ensures that decisions are made in the best interest of all parties.
- **How It Drives Profitability**: Transparent practices attract ESG-focused investors and prevent costly scandals.
- **Example**: **Patagonia** reports its environmental impact in detail, earning customer loyalty and driving revenue while staying true to its mission of sustainability.

b. Long-Term Decision-Making

- **Why It Matters**: Ethical governance prioritizes sustainable practices over short-term financial gains, aligning with stakeholder values.
- **How It Drives Profitability**: Companies that focus on long-term impacts are better positioned to weather market volatility.
- **Example**: **Tesla** invests heavily in renewable technologies, achieving profitability while advancing sustainability goals.

c. Ethical Leadership

- **Why It Matters**: Ethical leaders model behaviour that fosters a culture of integrity and responsibility.
- **How It Drives Profitability**: Employee retention improves, and customer trust increases, reducing costs and enhancing brand value.

- **Example: Starbucks** implements ethical sourcing and empowers employees with equitable pay, improving employee engagement and productivity.

d. ESG Integration

- **Why It Matters**: ESG integration ensures that environmental and social considerations are part of the governance framework.
- **How It Drives Profitability**: Aligning with ESG standards attracts investments and reduces risks associated with non-compliance.
- **Example: Microsoft** achieved carbon neutrality by embedding ESG principles into its governance, leading to increased investor confidence.

---

3. Implementing Ethical Governance

a. Establish Robust Policies

- Develop a comprehensive **Code of Ethics** and compliance frameworks that outline expectations for all stakeholders.
- **Example: Johnson & Johnson's Credo** guides decision-making during crises, such as the Tylenol recall, reinforcing trust and safeguarding the company's reputation.

b. Utilize Data and Technology

- Leverage analytics to monitor adherence to governance policies and ESG goals.
- **Example: Siemens** uses AI to enhance compliance checks, reducing the risk of governance violations.

c. Stakeholder Engagement

- Actively involve employees, investors, customers, and communities in decision-making.

- **Example**: **Shell** engages stakeholders to set sustainability goals, ensuring alignment with societal expectations.

d. Monitor and Audit

- Regular audits identify gaps in governance and sustainability efforts.
- **Example**: **Nestlé** conducts independent audits of its supply chain to maintain transparency and improve ethical sourcing.

4. Benefits of Ethical Governance

Benefit	Impact
Increased Stakeholder Trust	Builds loyalty among investors, customers, and employees.
Enhanced Financial Performance	ESG-aligned companies consistently outperform competitors financially.
Risk Mitigation	Reduces the likelihood of scandals, penalties, and reputational damage.
Sustainable Growth	Balances profit with environmental and social contributions.

5. Case Studies of Ethical Governance in Action

a. Tata Group

- **Initiative**: A governance framework emphasizing community welfare and sustainability.
- **Outcome**: Tata's ethical business practices ensure strong financial performance and enduring stakeholder trust.

b. Danone

- **Initiative**: Became an *Entreprise à Mission*, incorporating sustainability and health into its governance.

- **Outcome**: Improved market share and ESG ratings, attracting long-term investors.

c. **IKEA**
- **Initiative**: Integrated circular economy principles into governance, reducing waste and emissions.
- **Outcome**: Achieved profitability while positioning itself as a leader in sustainability.

Conclusion

Ethical governance is not just a moral imperative; it is a business strategy for ensuring profitability and sustainability. Companies that integrate integrity, transparency, and accountability into their governance frameworks can build long-term resilience, attract stakeholders, and drive innovation while contributing positively to society and the environment.

Inspiring Future Leaders to Redefine Management without Manipulation

In the evolving business world, leadership needs to transition from traditional, control-driven management to a model that emphasizes transparency, collaboration, and integrity. Future leaders should adopt ethical frameworks, build trust, and focus on sustainable growth while actively rejecting manipulative practices.

Core Principles to Redefine Management

1. Emphasize Ethical Leadership

- **Why It Matters:** Ethical leadership fosters a culture of trust and accountability.
- **How to Inspire:** Train leaders to prioritize long-term value over short-term gains by incorporating ethics into decision-making processes.

- **Example: Indra Nooyi** of PepsiCo redefined leadership by focusing on sustainability and corporate responsibility through the "Performance with Purpose" initiative.

2. Cultivate a Growth Mindset

- **Why It Matters:** Encouraging learning and adaptability helps leaders handle challenges with creativity and resilience.
- **How to Inspire:** Provide opportunities for continuous development, mentorship, and exposure to diverse viewpoints.
- **Example: Satya Nadella** transformed Microsoft's culture by embedding a growth mindset, focusing on innovation, inclusivity, and collaboration.

3. Build Transparent Communication Channels

- **Why It Matters:** Transparency reduces ambiguity and builds credibility among teams and stakeholders.
- **How to Inspire:** Promote open communication, regular feedback loops, and honest reporting mechanisms.
- **Example: Patagonia**'s transparent sustainability reports demonstrate how clear communication aligns organizational goals with stakeholder trust.

4. Focus on Collaboration Over Competition

- **Why It Matters:** Collaborative environments encourage collective problem-solving and shared success.
- **How to Inspire:** Implement team-based objectives, cross-functional projects, and reward collaboration over individual achievement.

- **Example: Google's Project Aristotle** revealed that psychological safety and collaboration are critical for high-performing teams.

---

5. Redefine Success Beyond Profit

- **Why It Matters:** Balancing financial goals with social and environmental responsibility ensures long-term impact.
- **How to Inspire:** Train leaders to use frameworks like ESG (Environmental, Social, Governance) and the Triple Bottom Line (People, Planet, Profit).
- **Example: Unilever** ties executive compensation to sustainability metrics, ensuring accountability for social and environmental goals.

Practical Steps to Inspire Future Leaders

1. **Leadership Development Programs:**
    - Incorporate ethics, emotional intelligence (EQ), and stakeholder management into executive training.
    - **Case Study:** Amazon's leadership principles emphasize customer obsession, ownership, and delivering results while maintaining integrity.
2. **Role Modelling by Current Leaders:**
    - Leaders should demonstrate accountability, inclusivity, and transparency.
    - **Example:** Howard Schultz, former CEO of Starbucks, consistently modelled servant leadership by prioritizing employee welfare and ethical sourcing.

3. **Mentorship and Coaching:**
   - Pair aspiring leaders with mentors who exemplify ethical and effective leadership.
   - Use structured feedback mechanisms to align their growth with organizational values.

4. **Scenario-Based Training:**
   - Use real-world case studies and simulations to teach leaders how to navigate ethical dilemmas and complex challenges.

5. **Fostering Innovation Without Exploitation:**
   - Encourage experimentation while ensuring that employee ideas are credited and valued.
   - **Example:** 3M's "15% Rule" allows employees to dedicate time to passion projects, fostering innovation and ownership.

Measuring the Impact of Redefined Leadership

Metric	What It Measures	How It Inspires Leaders
Employee Engagement Scores	Trust and satisfaction within the workforce.	Reflects the leader's ability to inspire and connect with teams.
ESG Performance Ratings	Alignment of organizational practices with sustainability.	Demonstrates commitment to ethical governance and global goals.
Innovation Metrics	Rate of successful innovations and idea implementation.	Highlights the leader's ability to foster creativity and collaboration.
Stakeholder Feedback	Trust and satisfaction among customers, investors, etc.	Validates the leader's alignment with broader organizational goals.

Long-Term Vision

Redefining management is not just about changing practices but also about inspiring a paradigm shift in leadership philosophy. Future leaders should prioritize ethical decision-making, inclusivity, and sustainable impact, creating organizations admired for integrity and resilience. This will ensure not only their organization's success but also their legacy **as Transformative Leaders.**

Redefining management in today's era demands a focus on ethical leadership that **avoids manipulation** and **discourages office politics** while **integrating Environmental, Social, and Governance (ESG) principles**. This approach **ensures accountability, inclusivity**, and **transparency**, fostering sustainable growth and stakeholder trust.

Core Strategies for Ethical Leadership

1. Eliminating Office Politics

- **Why It Matters:** Office politics undermines trust, reduces productivity, and creates a toxic work environment.
- **How to Inspire Leaders:**
    - **Merit-Based Systems:** Establish transparent criteria for promotions and rewards to reduce favouritism.
    - **Open Communication:** Encourage open-door policies and anonymous feedback mechanisms to address grievances.
    - **Vigilance in Leadership:** Train leaders to recognize and address signs of manipulation or favouritism within teams.
    - **Example:** Procter & Gamble fosters a meritocratic culture by emphasizing performance-based promotions and 360-degree reviews.

2. Embedding ESG Factors in Leadership

- **Why It Matters:** Integrating ESG principles aligns leadership decisions with global sustainability goals and ethical standards.
- **How to Inspire Leaders:**
    - Familiarize leaders with global ESG frameworks like **GRI**, **SASB**, **UN SDGs**, and **TCFD** reporting standards.
    - Embed ESG goals into business strategy and leadership KPIs.
    - Encourage cross-departmental collaboration to address ESG challenges holistically.
    - **Example:** Unilever ties executive compensation to progress on ESG metrics, ensuring leadership accountability.

3. Focusing on Transparent and Accountable Reporting

- **Why It Matters:** Transparent reporting reduces the risk of greenwashing or data manipulation, building stakeholder trust.
- **How to Inspire Leaders:**
    - Use standardized ESG reporting frameworks to maintain consistency and credibility.
    - Conduct regular audits to verify the accuracy of ESG disclosures.
    - Provide training on ethical reporting practices and risk management.
    - **Example:** Microsoft aligns its operations with TCFD recommendations, offering transparent climate risk disclosures.

Creating Vigilant ESG Leadership

a. ESG Education and Training

- Familiarize leaders with:
    - **GRI** (Global Reporting Initiative): Focuses on sustainability reporting.
    - **SASB** (Sustainability Accounting Standards Board): Links sustainability data to financial outcomes.
    - **TCFD** (Task Force on Climate-Related Financial Disclosures): Encourages transparency in climate risks.
    - **UN SDGs** (Sustainable Development Goals): Aligns organizational efforts with global development priorities.
- **Example:** Danone's "One Planet, One Health" integrates training on SDGs into its leadership development programs.

b. Building ESG-Integrated Goals

- Define business strategies that align profit with sustainable practices.
- Use metrics like carbon footprint reduction, diversity in leadership, and community impact for performance reviews.
- **Example:** IKEA's ESG-aligned goals include sourcing 100% renewable energy and reducing waste by embedding circular economy principles.

Avoiding Manipulation in ESG Reporting

1. **Strengthen Governance**: Establish independent committees to oversee ESG initiatives and reporting.
2. **Automate Data Collection**: Use technology like AI to ensure unbiased and consistent ESG data.

3. **Conduct Regular Audits**: Partner with third-party auditors to validate ESG disclosures.
4. **Stakeholder Engagement**: Actively involve employees, customers, and investors in ESG strategy formulation.

The Role of Ethical Leadership in ESG Integration

Case Study: Patagonia

- **Approach:** Demonstrates ethical governance by emphasizing environmental preservation and social equity.
- **Practices:** Transparent reporting on sustainability initiatives and proactive engagement with stakeholders.
- **Impact:** Positioned as a leader in ethical management, earning customer loyalty and driving profitability.

Case Study: Tesla

- **Approach:** Leadership-driven focus on renewable energy and carbon reduction.
- **Practices:** Disclosures aligned with TCFD recommendations and innovative sustainability initiatives.
- **Impact:** Increased investor confidence and market dominance in the EV industry.

Metrics to Inspire and Measure Leadership Success

Category	Metric	Impact
Eliminating Politics	Anonymous Employee Satisfaction Surveys	Indicates reduction in favouritism and workplace conflicts.
ESG Integration	Progress on GRI, SASB, and TCFD Metrics	Demonstrates alignment with global sustainability goals.
Stakeholder Trust	Investor Confidence Ratings	Reflects the credibility of ESG and governance initiatives.
Transparency and Reporting	Audit Scores and External Certifications	Validates the authenticity of ESG and operational data.

Long-Term Vision

Future leaders must redefine management by focusing on ethical practices, collaborative cultures, and ESG accountability. By fostering transparency, discouraging manipulation, and aligning leadership practices with global sustainability goals, organizations can create lasting value for stakeholders while ensuring resilience in a rapidly changing world.

Epilogue: The Path to Sustainable Success

Reflecting on the true purpose of management

A call to action for leaders, HR professionals, and stakeholders

The Path to Sustainable Success

The journey toward sustainable success is not defined by short-term wins or fleeting triumphs but by enduring principles that align growth with ethical governance, integrity, and responsibility. As organizations navigate a complex, fast-changing world, the emphasis on sustainability, transparency, and inclusivity becomes the cornerstone of long-term value creation.

Building a Legacy Through Ethical Leadership

Sustainable success requires leaders who champion accountability, foster trust, and set a vision that transcends immediate gains. These leaders inspire through actions rooted in authenticity, encouraging organizations to balance profitability with positive societal impact.

- **Example:** Indra Nooyi's leadership at PepsiCo emphasized "Performance with Purpose," showcasing how companies can achieve financial success while addressing societal and environmental needs.

The Role of Integrity and Innovation

A sustainable path forward rejects manipulation and short-sighted practices in favour of innovation and ethical strategies. Integrity-driven organizations build resilient cultures where innovation thrives without compromising core values.

- **Example:** Unilever's commitment to sustainability through its Sustainable Living Plan has enhanced brand loyalty while driving consistent financial performance.

Aligning with Global Sustainability Goals

True success is measured by an organization's contribution to the greater good. Aligning strategies with global frameworks such as the UN's Sustainable Development Goals (SDGs) and ESG reporting standards ensures accountability to stakeholders and the environment.

- **Example:** Tesla's mission to accelerate the world's transition to sustainable energy exemplifies the integration of profitability and global responsibility.

The Future Belongs to the Ethical

Organizations that build cultures of learning, transparency, and collaboration are not just creating a better workplace—they are preparing for a future where success is measured by both economic impact and societal progress.

As the curtain closes on this exploration of redefined management, one truth emerges: sustainable success is not a destination but a continuous journey. By rejecting manipulation, embracing integrity, and fostering inclusive growth, organizations and leaders pave the way for a thriving, equitable, and sustainable future.

The path forward is clear lead with purpose, act with integrity, and innovate for the betterment of all. This is the legacy of sustainable success.

Reflecting on the True Purpose of Management

Management is more than just overseeing resources, meeting deadlines, and achieving targets; it is the art and science of aligning people, processes, and goals to create value. At its core, management serves a deeper purpose that transcends operational efficiency—it is about inspiring growth, fostering innovation, and ensuring sustainability for all stakeholders.

1. Enabling People to Thrive

- **True Purpose:** Management is fundamentally about enabling individuals and teams to realize their potential. This involves creating an environment where people feel valued, supported, and empowered to contribute their best.

- **Example:** Companies like Google emphasize psychological safety and inclusivity, ensuring teams feel safe to express ideas and take risks.

2. Achieving Collective Goals

- **True Purpose:** Management coordinates efforts to achieve collective goals that would be unattainable through individual contributions alone. This includes aligning personal objectives with organizational vision.

- **Example:** Toyota's lean management philosophy focuses on teamwork and continuous improvement to achieve operational excellence while respecting each team member's role.

3. Fostering Ethical and Sustainable Practices

- **True Purpose:** Effective management ensures that organizational practices align with ethical values and sustainability principles. It considers the long-term impact on the environment, society, and economy.

- **Example:** Patagonia embeds environmental stewardship in its operations, demonstrating how management can drive ethical decision-making and sustainability.

4. Balancing Innovation and Stability

- **True Purpose:** Management must strike a balance between maintaining operational stability and fostering innovation. It ensures the organization remains competitive while safeguarding its core values and processes.
- **Example:** Apple blends disciplined product management with innovative design, consistently delivering groundbreaking products without losing focus on quality.

5. Acting as Stewards of Resources

- **True Purpose:** Management is entrusted with optimizing resources, including human capital, finances, and materials, for maximum efficiency and value creation.
- **Example:** Unilever's Sustainable Living Plan demonstrates how responsible management can optimize resources for profitability and sustainability.

6. Inspiring Leadership

- **True Purpose:** Management is not just about controlling or directing but about inspiring teams to pursue shared visions with passion and dedication.
- **Example:** Starbucks CEO Howard Schultz built a culture of purpose by emphasizing employee welfare, ethical sourcing, and community engagement.

7. Adapting to Change

- **True Purpose:** In an ever-changing world, management ensures organizations remain adaptable and resilient, prepared to navigate uncertainty and seize opportunities.
- **Example:** Microsoft's transformation under Satya Nadella showcased the power of adaptive leadership, emphasizing a growth mindset to embrace digital transformation.

Key Insights on Management's Purpose

1. **Beyond Profits:** While profitability is crucial, the ultimate purpose of management includes building trust, fostering inclusivity, and driving positive societal impact.
2. **Holistic Focus:** Management integrates people, processes, and technology to create value across economic, environmental, and social dimensions.
3. **Legacy Building:** By aligning daily operations with ethical and sustainable principles, management contributes to a legacy of resilience and purpose-driven success.

Reflecting on the true purpose of management invites us to view it as a means of uplifting not only organizations but also the people and communities they serve. True management is a stewardship of potential, driving progress with integrity and vision.

A call to action for Leaders, HR professionals, and Stakeholders

As organizations navigate an era defined by rapid change, increasing complexity, and growing societal expectations, it is imperative for leaders, HR professionals, and stakeholders to unite in creating a future that is ethical, inclusive, and sustainable. Here's how each group can contribute:

For Leaders: Guiding with Vision and Integrity

- **Commit to Ethical Governance**: Lead by example, embedding transparency and accountability in all decisions.
    - **Actionable Steps**: Implement and uphold robust ethical frameworks like the UN SDGs, GRI, and TCFD to align corporate strategies with global sustainability goals.
- **Drive Innovation and Adaptability**: Encourage a growth mindset, invest in technology, and foster a culture of continuous learning to prepare for future challenges.
    - **Example**: Leaders like Satya Nadella have transformed companies by promoting adaptability and ethical innovation.
- **Champion Stakeholder Value**: Redefine success beyond profits, focusing on creating long-term value for customers, employees, investors, and communities.

For HR Professionals: Building Resilient and Inclusive Workforces

- **Develop Competency-Based Frameworks**: Design systems that align skills development with strategic goals, ensuring fairness and transparency in recruitment and performance management.
    - **Actionable Steps**: Use unbiased tools for skill assessments and introduce continuous learning programs tailored to evolving business needs.

- **Cultivate Inclusive Cultures**: Create environments where diversity thrives, and employees feel empowered to contribute authentically.
    - **Example**: Procter & Gamble emphasizes equity through its hiring and leadership development programs.
- **Conduct Culture Audits**: Regularly evaluate organizational culture to identify and address gaps in alignment with core values and ethics.
    - **Impact**: Enhances employee engagement and reduces turnover.

For Stakeholders: Advocating for Accountability and Impact

- **Demand ESG Transparency**: Hold organizations accountable for their environmental, social, and governance performance through active engagement and advocacy.
    - **Actionable Steps**: Monitor companies' ESG disclosures via standards like SASB and TCFD to ensure alignment with sustainable practices.
- **Support Ethical Companies**: Invest in organizations that prioritize integrity and sustainability, amplifying their impact while ensuring long-term returns.
    - **Example**: Tesla's commitment to sustainability has attracted a loyal base of ESG-conscious investors.
- **Collaborate for Change**: Partner with organizations to co-create solutions for societal challenges, leveraging shared resources and expertise.

The Collective Vision

1. **Leaders**: Set the tone for ethical and transformative practices.
2. **HR Professionals**: Build the systems and cultures needed to sustain these practices.
3. **Stakeholders**: Hold organizations accountable, ensuring alignment with societal and environmental goals.

The Time is Now

The challenges we face—from climate change to inequality—require immediate action. Together, leaders, HR professionals, and stakeholders can redefine the purpose of business to drive meaningful, lasting impact. Let this be the call to step forward, to act with purpose, and to build a world where success is measured not just by profits but by progress for all.

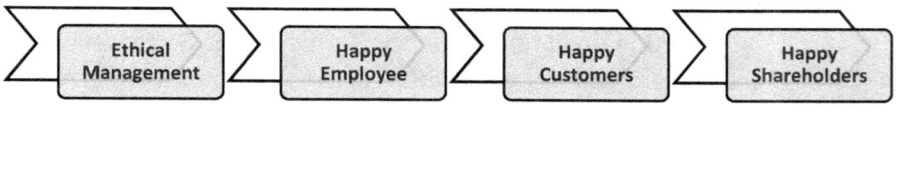

For Training Enquiry mail at: **augustalent@outlook.com**

References:

Books and Reports

1. **World Economic Forum**
    - "The Future of Jobs Report 2023" – Insight into skill transformation and workforce readiness in evolving markets.

2. **John Elkington**
    - "Cannibals with Forks: The Triple Bottom Line of 21st Century Business" – Foundational work on the Triple Bottom Line (People, Planet, Profit).

3. **Harvard Business Review**
    - Various articles on ethical leadership, organizational behaviour, and adaptive management strategies.

Corporate Case Studies and Initiatives

1. **Unilever's Sustainable Living Plan**
    - Details on integrating ESG goals into corporate strategy.

2. **Tesla's ESG Reporting and Climate Strategy**
    - Use of TCFD recommendations to disclose climate-related risks and opportunities.

3. **Microsoft's Leadership Transformation under Satya Nadella**
    - Case studies highlighting growth mindset and ethical innovation.

4. **Johnson & Johnson Credo**
    - The role of ethical frameworks during crises like the Tylenol recall.

Standards and Frameworks

1. **ESG Reporting Standards**
    - **Global Reporting Initiative (GRI):** Sustainability metrics and disclosures.
    - **Sustainability Accounting Standards Board (SASB):** Industry-specific sustainability reporting.
    - **Task Force on Climate-Related Financial Disclosures (TCFD):** Guidelines for climate risk reporting.

- United Nations Sustainable Development Goals (UN SDGs): Global framework for sustainable development.

2. **Balanced Scorecard (BSC)**
   - Strategic tool for aligning financial and non-financial goals with business strategy.

Corporate Governance and Compliance

1. **Siemens Compliance Systems**
   - Post-scandal governance restructuring for enhanced transparency.
2. **Patagonia's Transparency Model**
   - Reporting on environmental and social impact to build customer loyalty.

Leadership Development and Organizational Culture

1. **Google's Project Oxygen and Project Aristotle**
   - Research on high-performing teams and leadership qualities.
2. **Procter & Gamble's Leadership Programs**
   - Building a culture of meritocracy and performance-driven management.

Tools and Techniques

1. **GE-McKinsey 9-Box Framework**
   - Tool for talent assessment and development.
2. **Net Promoter Score (NPS) and Voice of Customer (VOC)**
   - Tools for customer and employee feedback to improve services and culture.
3. **Lean Management and Toyota Production System (TPS)**
   - Operational frameworks to optimize efficiency and quality.

Digital Learning and Transformation

1. **AT&T Workforce 2020**
   - Case study on re-skilling employees for digital transformation.

2. **IBM SkillsBuild Initiative**
   - Training programs for emerging technologies like AI and blockchain.

Ethical Leadership and Decision-Making

1. **Indra Nooyi's "Performance with Purpose"**
   - Focus on ethical leadership and sustainability.
2. **Howard Schultz and Starbucks' Servant Leadership**
   - Case study on prioritizing employee welfare and ethical sourcing.

Key Websites

1. Global Reporting Initiative (GRI)
2. Task Force on Climate-Related Financial Disclosures (TCFD)
3. Sustainability Accounting Standards Board (SASB)
4. United Nations Sustainable Development Goals (UN SDGs)

Academic Journals and Articles

1. Articles from **McKinsey Quarterly**, **Harvard Business Review**, and **Forbes** on ethical leadership, ESG integration, and innovation in business management.
2. Reports by **World Economic Forum** on workforce trends and the future of management.

www.ingramcontent.com/pod-product-compliance
Lightning Source LLC
Chambersburg PA
CBHW071021240526
45469CB00006BD/2032